IN THE MIDDLE OF THE WOOD

IN THE MIDDLE OF THE WOOD

A NOVEL

by

IAIN CRICHTON SMITH

LONDON
VICTOR GOLLANCZ LTD
1987

First published in Great Britain 1987
by Victor Gollancz Ltd,
14 Henrietta Street, London WC2E 8QJ

ACKNOWLEDGEMENT

The quotation opposite, from Dante's *Inferno*,
is translated by the Rev. Francis Cary.

British Library Cataloguing in Publication Data
Smith, Iain Crichton
In the middle of the wood.
I. Title
823'.914[F]   PR6005.R58

ISBN 0-575-03967-1

Typeset at The Spartan Press Ltd,
Lymington, Hants
and printed in Great Britain by
St Edmundsbury Press Ltd, Bury St Edmunds, Suffolk

In the midway of this our mortal life,
I found me in a gloomy wood, astray,
Gone from the path direct . . .

For Muriel and
Alick John Macleod,
true & trusted friends.

One

VICIOUSLY HE THRUST his manuscripts and clothes into his case and before his wife, Linda, knew what he was doing he was making his way down to the station. He knew now that the house was evil and that he must get away from it, lest it should destroy him. She had already torn in half the telephone book which lay on his desk in the study and had also shuffled with demonic hatred for him the pages of his new novel over which he had been stalled for a considerable time. No, there was nothing for him here: if he stayed he would lose his sanity. He felt that there was witchcraft in the house, that a spell had been cast on him, that the world was falling apart and that the centre wouldn't hold. He slammed the door shut behind him. Linda was hanging up clothes on the clothes line: they looked like a gallery of paintings.

He walked from the house and crossed the railway line with its rusty tracks, alongside which red weeds were brilliantly flowering, and in the grass to his right he saw rabbits playing in the fields. He looked around him as if he were seeing the place for the last time and must memorize it. The house, his and Linda's, shone white against the red and the green: the brown tiles of its roof slanted over the ghostly walls. Now more than ever it seemed to him to be a witch house. As he walked he felt hot and sweaty: when he got on to the train he would have to remove his jacket. More and more now he broke out into these sweats: not so long ago in a bookshop in Glasgow he had felt the perspiration pouring from him so that he had to leave and remove his jacket and find a toilet where he could plunge his head into a basin of cold water. He put his left hand into his pocket and took out three of the red pills, which he thrust into his mouth. He devoured pills like sweets these days.

He crossed the railway-line and made his way to the bench which was on the opposite side of the tracks, the platform from which the Glasgow train would leave. He sat down on it. He knew that he had two hours to wait but he didn't care: he would rather wait here than in the house. He stared across at the newspaper kiosk and saw Maggie standing behind the counter. As he watched he saw Rhona Macintyre, dressed in slacks and a cream blouse, walking along to the kiosk. She stopped there and she and Maggie began to talk to each other. It seemed that they were talking about him, so clear and supernaturally alert his hearing had become. Now and again Rhona would turn round and look over directly to where he was sitting. The two of them would obviously be wondering why he should be waiting on a platform for a train that wouldn't arrive for two hours. But in fact he didn't care whether they talked about him or not. He had his manuscripts and his clothes and that was all he needed. When he arrived in Glasgow he would find lodgings, perhaps in a house or in a hotel. A hotel might be better for then he could go straight to his bed and sleep: he wanted to sleep for days, weeks, forever.

And then as he thought about that he remembered that he hadn't taken his typewriter with him. He should really have remembered to do that: he might now have to buy one and that was extravagant when he had one already. How had he not realized that he didn't have his typewriter: how had he not missed it? Of course he had been in such a hurry cramming his case with manuscripts and clothes that he couldn't think of everything. And the decision had been a sudden one. One moment he was sitting at his desk staring out of the window, the telephone at his right hand, and the next he was frenziedly packing his case. It was almost as if a voice had spoken to him and told him, You must get out of this house at once, without a second's delay. And that was precisely what he had done: and now on this warm day he was sitting on a bench waiting for a train to arrive.

Rhona was still there talking animatedly to Maggie. He knew that they were talking about him. For one thing he didn't usually travel by train. He was always sitting at his desk writing, day after day, while people passing on the road could see him through the window. It was important to him that he should not appear idle to them, that he should be seen as either typing or reading. In a village like this people would think you lazy when they didn't see you working. And in any case it was hard enough for them to understand someone who wrote for a living. He was a mysterious being to them. They themselves either had jobs in the neighbouring town or they worked on the land. But they didn't have anyone else in the village who earned his living in such an obscure way. And he felt that if they once saw him idle they would assume that he was like that all the time, such was the obvious simplicity of their minds.

He relaxed in the sunshine and closed his eyes wearily, after drawing his case towards him and holding it between his legs. If he lost his manuscripts he would have lost everything. As he did so he noticed his wife in their red car pulling up at the station. He turned his eyes away and stared obstinately in the other direction. He heard the car door slam and then her footsteps crossing the rails towards him. Then she was standing beside him, dressed in her velvet jacket and skirt.

"Where are you going?" she asked.

He didn't answer.

"Look," she said. "You must come home. The train doesn't leave for another two hours anyway. What's wrong with you?"

Still he didn't answer. He felt that if he answered he would be submitting to her. She was a cunning witch, she was making sure that the two women at the book-stall knew that she had tried her best, but that he was having none of it. No, he wouldn't speak to her, that was certain. On no account. Suddenly he thrust his left hand ahead of him and looked at it. He wished to know whether his fingers were still trembling. They were, three of them, trembling like compass needles.

"All right then," said Linda. "All right then. If that is the way you want it." Then she walked away. Rhona and Maggie were turned from the two of them, pretending to be deep in a mysterious conversation of their own, but he knew that they were listening, that they were following everything with rapt attention. There was not a word that they would not be able to reproduce.

He had made so many mistakes since he had come to that village. For instance, he hadn't understood how much gossip was necessary to the lives of the people nor had he spoken to the villagers as much as he should have done. A village was not like a town or a city. In the city random roads crossed continually, there were creative collisions on streets which one might not see again. But in the village the roads were fixed from time immemorial, there were few surprises. Ruts were bitten deep into time, there was a continual re-creation of the past in the present. And then again he had felt so self-conscious, so sure that people were watching him all the time, and he had made unusually many errors, especially at the post office.

He watched Linda climb into her car, and then she started it and was gone. For a moment he felt a pang of regret as if he would never see her again, but then the regret was replaced by anger. She should have known what would happen. Why had she torn his telephone book in two, why had she shuffled his papers? She was jealous of him, that was what it was. She was just an ordinary person, he on the other hand was an extraordinary person, and the ordinary must hate the extraordinary. He couldn't live in the ordinary, its gaunt plumageless sky. He couldn't understand how ordinary people lived. It seemed to him that their lives were so bare and dull, that they had no excitement, no hope, no future. Nothing but a vacuum filled only by conversation. And then Linda was always asking him to talk to her, it was as if she could not exist unless she was conversing. And most of the time he felt no inclination to talk. In fact he hated talking. He preferred books to people, that was quite clear to him. Why should he spend time chattering about trivial matters to trivial people when there was a book by Plato or Tolstoy to be read? Ordinary conversation was so untidy, it had not been turned into art, it had not been revised. And he was not interested in births, deaths and marriages, in babies, engagements, divorces.

Now he could see Ina coming. And he knew that she and Maggie were talking about him though Ina was careful not to turn round and look at him. There was still a considerable time before the train was due and the villagers were all wondering what he was doing sitting on the bench so early. The news would be round the whole village by now. Oh, certainly it would be, quite obviously.

He felt cooler now and glad of it. He hated it when he sweated just as he had done in his childhood when he had suffered from bronchitis. He stretched his legs out comfortably in front of him and closed his eyes. As he did so it seemed to him that he could hear Ina talking about him, that she was saying that he was an odd sort of person, not suited to the village. That was the unfair part: they didn't know that Linda had torn his telephone book and shuffled up the pages of his novel, and of course he wouldn't tell them. No, he might tell them now, though in the past he had been very taciturn, believing that it was a kind of treachery to talk about family affairs. But he would tell them now, he would tell them exactly what Linda was like, that she had torn his telephone book in half (what angry superhuman strength she must have had), that she had even shifted some of the vases in order to confuse him. She was undoubtedly trying to draw him into the morass of her own ordinariness, he was the pheasant with the coloured wings while she was the hen clucking about a great empty yard.

And there she was again at the station in her car, having returned. But this time she didn't get out of it. She sat in it and looked forlornly across to him but he knew that this forlornness was a mask which she had assumed. He stared back at her in a hostile manner. He wanted to have nothing more to do with her. The fact was that she was frightened that he would reveal her tricks in his next book, how she had shifted the vases and the furniture, and shuffled the pages of his book. And by God he would reveal it. Already he had the plot in his mind. She would be the barbarian who hated the disciplines of art, who hid the vases out of chicanery. Oh, he would really fix her this time, no question of that.

And yet he had loved her too. He could think this with infinite regret as he stared back at the car with an unsmiling face. Together they used to go out for dinner every Saturday to a different hotel. Before that they had driven to their favourite glen where they sat watching the dark flow of the water, with flowers here and there on the bank and deer peering down from the hills with their frail questioning heads. Oh, he had loved her, and if they quarrelled he would have a sleepless night and in the morning buy a huge extravagant bouquet of flowers for her. It was she who had taught him to be jealous; before that he had lived in mornings clear of human passions. But then for a long while he wouldn't let men talk to her. He suspected her of the most terrible things, of betraying him continually. She was the frightening Eve of his imagination, the snake in the garden.

And now she had made up her mind and was crossing the railway line again. But he didn't want to go with her in the car. He knew that she would try to entice him back to the house if he entered the car. And above all he didn't want that, he didn't want to go back to that house ever. It had almost destroyed him. That was yet another of her tricks, she was full of cunning subterfuges, oh, there was never anyone like her for trickery.

"Where are you thinking of going?" she asked.

"Glasgow," he answered.

"All right then," she said. "I'll take you in the car if that is what you want to do."

"No," he said with finality.

She stood and looked at him, and then she said, "You know if I leave you this time I won't come back."

"Yes," he said with the same dead finality.

"I see." And before he could say any more she was striding purposefully away. This time he felt sure that she would not return, and he didn't care.

He heard the car door slamming and almost shouted to her but then gritted his teeth and didn't do so. He stared down at his feet, then at the kiosk, then across to the chugging goods-train on the other line. Well, if that was what she wanted, that was it. He knew that it had to come, he had felt the autumnal scent of their parting some time ago, it had been like gunnery on the horizon. And yet how was it that she looked like a refugee, as she walked away from him through the dust of summer? She was nowhere to be seen and the silence descended again.

About twenty minutes before the train was due to leave, a man came and sat beside him on the bench. It was a big heavy man and he couldn't remember having seen him about the village though that of course was no guarantee that he was a stranger. He looked like a man from the city, not from the village, he looked like . . . well, he looked like a Glasgow thug. And yet he was well dressed enough, he wore a tweedy suit and a white shirt and tie. But he didn't have a case, that was what Ralph noticed particularly. If he was a visitor to the village why was he not carrying a case? And, furthermore, as he sat there with his big hands resting on his knees he made Ralph uneasy. He looked so calm, so easy, so able to take care of himself in any situation. Again, he had a broken nose or if not a broken nose what looked like a boxer's nose. A big hefty man with a boxer's nose, no case, wearing a black tie with a tweedy suit. There was an oddity, an eccentricity, about him, and yet he appeared fixed exactly in his flesh, in his mind, solid and heavy and relaxed.

He didn't speak to Ralph at all. He simply sat like a statue with his big hands resting heavily on his knees. If he had been a villager he was bound to have spoken, to have said, "It's a fine day", to have handed over the worn coinage of the weather, but, no, he had no intention of speaking. And yet there was no uneasiness in his silence, though Ralph felt uneasy.

Once he turned his gaze full on Ralph and smiled. The smile

bothered Ralph, it was almost a knowing smile, not a full open smile at all. It was as if he was saying to him, "I know you. I know you for what you are. I on the other hand am stronger than you. I could break you in two quite easily, and it wouldn't bother me in the least." It was as if he were on a mission which he was confident of accomplishing but which he had not yet begun. Ralph shook his head like a dog emerging from water and stared fixedly at the signal, which was down. The train wouldn't be long now.

And then as he was gazing at the signal he heard a car arriving at the station again. He looked and it was Linda. She got out of the car and ran lightly across the line carrying a case, and then she was standing beside him.

"If you don't want to come in the car I'll go with you on the train," she said.

The man on the bench made no sign that he had heard and yet Ralph could have sworn that he had glanced at his wife in a meaningful way, and that she had answered his glance. There is more to this than meets the eye, he thought, why has she decided to come with me? Maybe she has telephoned someone, I wouldn't put it past her, her cunning is past belief. He had the definite feeling that the two of them, this man and Linda, knew each other. And he didn't care whether she came to Glasgow with him or not. If that was what she wanted to do let her do it. How calm and peaceful this station was with its flowers glowing in the sunlight and the blue paint shining in the light. It was as if he was leaving a heaven that he would never see again.

He didn't answer his wife. If she wanted to come that was up to her. At least she intended staying with him, perhaps in the same hotel or the same boarding house, for she had hastily packed a case. He was determined not to speak to anyone: actually it was an effort for him to talk. It was as if he had to heave language from the bottom of a languid mysterious sea entangled with seaweed. He was too tired to use words. Words were what deceived people, not united them. She had deceived him: even now she was deceiving him, he couldn't trust her. And all the time the big man with the boxer's nose sat in silence and stared down at the gravel, his hands resting on his knees. Linda too remained silent. Perhaps she was astonished that he had not made a scene. Indeed, this was what this was, a scene, he felt, a piece of theatre. And he was sweating again. He hated when he sweated, he felt so unclean. And, again, to sweat was a weakness, it showed his vulnerability.

He wouldn't speak to her all the way down to Glasgow, he would show himself as the strong silent man. What was happening to him had gone beyond language, he no longer had anything to say to Linda. Women were a source of evil in the world, they were less straightforward, more complicated than men. Compared with women men were little boys playing in the illusive sun. He had had enough of that, more than enough. From now on he would be on his own, dependent on no one, there would be no trickery in his life, he would start afresh, he would have a new gaunt trembling origin.

When the train came and slowed down at the platform he carried his case into a compartment near the engine. He heaved it up to the rack and sat down in a corner seat. The big hefty man followed him into the same compartment and sat opposite him, and he was followed by Linda. There was also another man in the compartment, a thin man with a scar on his brow. The thin man smiled at the hefty man and then at Linda and suddenly took the case from her and placed it on the rack beside his own.

Ralph felt trapped, especially when the hefty man shut the door of the compartment. He could see quite clearly that there was some understanding between Linda and the other two men who, he was certain, also knew each other. They all sat in silence, the hefty man staring across at Ralph and smiling now and again. The thin man had started talking to Linda and was telling her about going to visit his sick wife in Glasgow where apparently she was in hospital. Also they had had a baby quite recently. But Ralph knew that all this was a pose. The thin man didn't have a baby or a wife in hospital, he was quite sure of that. The thin man with the scar on his brow — relic probably of a knife fight — was in fact a thug like the hefty man.

He saw the thin man looking at him oddly and then heard Linda whispering to him rapidly. What was she telling him? That he was mad? That he had tried to kill her? Or was she giving him instructions? The thin man listened intently, his head bent down towards Linda; his attention was almost painful to watch. Ralph made as if to open the door to the corridor but the hefty man smiled and shook his head. So that was it then. There definitely was a plot against him.

And then Ralph noticed a detail that he hadn't seen before. The window to the corridor was covered with a black blind which had been drawn downwards, so that it looked like a black shroud. The four of them were in fact locked in this compartment and no one walking along the corridor could see in, no matter what happened.

There was a deep odd silence in the compartment. The hefty man was sitting quietly and relaxedly with his hands folded in his lap, quite at ease, quite assured and confident. The thin man was staring straight ahead of him. It was as if they were all waiting for something to happen, Ralph was quite convinced of this. He had never seen a black curtain on the window of a train before now except at night. And then again it seemed to him that there was a connection between the curtain, and the black tie that the hefty man was wearing. It snaked down his shirt. Was he wearing it in honour of Ralph's death? Why should anyone wear a black tie with a tweedy suit and, furthermore, if he had been at a funeral and was returning to Glasgow after it, one would have expected him to have a case.

No, what had happened was quite clear to him. Linda had employed these two thugs in order to get rid of him. She had had plenty of time to phone, at least for the thin man, and presumably she had already given him his instructions. First, she had tried to drive him mad and failing to do that she was now trying to get rid of him. How had he not seen that so clearly before? It was because murder for him belonged to another world, not to his own world, perhaps to a city like Glasgow. And yet the newspapers were full of women who hired thugs to kill their husbands. It was true that they had often quarrelled in the past — Linda in fact despised him — but it had never occurred to him before that she would want to kill him. He looked sideways at her and studied her profile. Of course she was very strong-minded, for instance she had refused to have children, and nothing he could have said would have persuaded her otherwise. Not that he himself cared all that much for children as such, but it would have been a new experience. What was a writer without children? He was missing the common world with all its troubles and its complications. Oh, he had learned a lot from watching other people's children, but that wasn't the same, of course not.

It was quite clear to him that she was tired of him, she had perhaps been attracted at first by the unusual nature of his work but had then discovered that he was essentially a boring ordinary person after all. He could never understand why she had married him: but now she was intent on cancelling that error much as she would cancel an error in her typing, like the secretary which she had once been. How had he never understood before how implacably cold her mind was?

He stared at the black curtain on the window and thought to himself, The two of them will knock me out, perhaps strangle me, and then they will leave the train, or shift compartments. No one will see them because of the black curtain. Or they might even open the door and throw me out of the train. Already he felt his body rolling down a slope as it arched out of the train, and could see Linda watching it as if it were the end of a shoddy rainbow. Though she and the scarred man were chatting about the latter's wife and baby, he was quite sure that all that was a pose. It was a subtle con: she was only pretending to be interested in the baby, if baby there was, which he doubted. Why, if she were so interested in babies, did she not have one of her own?

He listened to the noise made by the train. It wasn't the usual rhythm. In fact it seemed to hum to itself the tune 'When You and I Were Young, Maggie', which was one of his favourite songs. He didn't understand why this should be since he wasn't a sentimental person and usually despised such songs and tunes.

'In days of long long ago. . . .'
the train beat out in repetitive rhythm.

The words brought back to him the times he and Linda, in the innocence of their courtship, had had dinner in many different hotels at weekends, and then late at night had watched Cannon on television, when they would together drink wine, or he whisky and she gin. The tune bothered him, he couldn't get it out of his head. The noise of the train was becoming louder and louder. He put his hands on his head and squeezed it, like a large soft fruit, between his hands, while the hefty man smiled at him and Linda and the thin man talked endlessly, chattering like water. The black tie of the hefty man reminded him of the black water of the river beside which they had often had a picnic, and that in turn reminded him of a phone, black and changing like liquid. The water itself was like an unintelligible conversation on a phone.

He mustn't stay where he was, that was certain. He must get out, or he would go mad. It seemed to him that one or other of the men had a small cassette in his pocket and was playing the tune that so much obsessed him. But how had they known that he liked it so much? It must have been Linda who had told them.

Suddenly, before he could think, he had slid open the door and in one rapid movement was out in the corridor and walking hastily along it. He thought of locking himself in the lavatory but didn't do so. No, they might have some method of getting into the lavatory with skeleton keys perhaps. Perhaps he would be better showing himself to other people so that they would remember him. As he stood in the corridor he heard the door of the compartment opening and turned to see that it was Linda. He stared at her in a hostile manner without speaking and walked further down the train. He took out a cigarette and lit it and looked out at the landscape in which cows grazed peacefully, while rivers tumbled headlong from the hills. He carefully shut the window of the door and kept well away from it, all the time looking about him in case the hefty man had crept up behind him without his noticing.

Where was Linda? Had she gone back to her compartment? Was she at this very moment gnashing her teeth with rage because she hadn't succeeded in her purpose, because he had seen through her plot? And then he saw her. She was standing beside one of the doors of the train. It might all be a trick. She might be enticing him towards the door so that the two men could come up behind him and throw him out. He gestured to her to come towards him, but she didn't move, and didn't seem to have noticed him. How cunning she was! She was obviously trying to show the other passengers that all this was his fault, that he was mad, that he was torturing her. But she wouldn't get away with that, he would be as cunning as she was. He put his hand hypocritically on her shoulder, smiling at her at the same time, but she drew away from him, staring at him as if she had never seen him before. He had better be careful or she might pretend that he had attacked her. Her trickery was inventive and infinite.

"What are you trying to do?" she whispered to him fiercely.

"What are *you* trying to do to me?" he whispered back to her. "Who are these two men?"

"What two men?"

"The two men in the compartment. Don't tell me that you don't know them."

"I have never seen them before in my life."

"You can tell that to a child. I am not a child. What do you think I am? Stupid?"

"I never thought you were stupid."

"What else do you think I am? What were you doing before you came to the train? Phoning?"

"I wasn't phoning. Strangely enough, I was packing. That was what I was doing."

"And before that?"

"I phoned your doctor. But he was away."

"And?"

"Nothing else."

He gazed at her with hatred. She had an answer for everything. God damn you, he muttered under his breath. How did I not notice before that you loathed me?

"You think being a writer is the most important thing on earth," she used to say to him. "What about doctors, nurses? Many of them never have their names quoted in magazines. All you want is letters. If you don't get letters you feel that the world has forgotten about you. Who do you think you are? You tell me that."

"No one in particular."

"That's not true. You think you are more important than Christ himself. You think you are better than Christ. Who do you think you really are?"

At that moment he saw the hefty man walking down the corridor towards him and he ducked into the nearest compartment. There was a man and a woman sitting there, the man reading a newspaper and the woman a book. They seemed respectable, remote, middle-class.

"My name is Ralph Simmons," he said. "What is your name?" The man stared at him in astonishment through his glasses. But Ralph wanted both of them to remember his name in case something happened to him. If the following day there was a little piece in the paper, that he had thrown himself out of the train, he wanted them to know that he had been perfectly sane, not at all suicidal.

"I'm going to Glasgow," he said. "I'm a writer. It's a glorious day, isn't it? Don't you feel that the summer has come at last?" He wished to impress on them that he was perfectly happy, perfectly normal, so that when the inspector of police examined them they would be able to say, "He seemed perfectly well-adjusted to us. He talked about the weather and did not seem worried in any way."

He took his bank book out of his pocket. "That is my name, there," he said to the man who was still staring at him in amazement. "I hope you'll remember me." Linda came in from the corridor and sat down opposite him. He pretended that he didn't know her. What had she come into this compartment for? Was she in fact trying to undermine his new tactic of convincing these two that he wasn't suicidal? He wouldn't put it past her.

He felt restless again and left the compartment. These two would remember him clearly enough if they read any story in the newspaper about him. He had fixed himself in their minds. Standing in the corridor he was aware of Linda behind him but he did not turn and look at her. He was trembling with rage. Why was she following him about? He opened the door of a long open compartment and stood there looking in, watching and being watched. As long as he stood there in full view, nothing would happen to him. He would stand there till the train had entered Glasgow.

And then a thought struck him. What was going to happen about his case? His case was still in the compartment where the two men were. It was on the rack opposite the hefty man. And it contained his manuscripts. Of course he couldn't leave the case there, he must not lose his manuscripts. He thought steadily with corrugated brow. Why, he must look like an ape or a monkey in a zoo, almost a man but not quite.

Maybe, then, he considered, I should leave the case on the rack till the two men have left the train when it arrives at its destination. But as soon as he had thought of this solution, he as soon dismissed it from his mind. For example, if he waited behind, the two men might wait behind as well, and they would attack him on a train shorn of all living beings except the three of them. No, that was no solution. After all people in Glasgow didn't pay any attention to you: you could be murdered on the road in broad daylight and the pedestrians would pass you by. He imagined himself being chased up and down the empty train till the two men had cornered him and taken his manuscripts, and killed him. Linda would want the manuscripts destroyed, that would be her revenge.

23

No, he mustn't do that. What then was the alternative? Well, could he not leave at an intervening station with his case, and then perhaps take a bus or another train to Glasgow? All he would have to do would be to wait till the last minute at the door, and then jump down to the platform as the train was pulling out of a station. How surprised they would be. Of course they might jump off the train at the next station and come back to look for him but by that time he would have thought of another trick. On the other hand, such a ruse would mean that he would have to go and get his case, and he didn't want to return to that compartment, not as long as these men were in it.

He committed his whole mind to the problem, thinking out all the possible angles. Linda always said that he was like a Hamlet —she had acted in the play at school — and that he never made up his mind about anything: she accused him of leaving all the major decisions to her. And that was true too but it was true only because he had a more complicated mind: her own mind on the contrary was always very simple and direct. He was amazed at the directness of it, how solutions were immediately presented to it. He himself had no common sense at all, he only had uncommon sense, or so he explained it to himself. He was not at all a practical person, and now he was being asked to be practical, to save his life by being so.

He knew that his life was at risk, he was quite clear about that. And it astonished him that she should hate him so much as to hire people to kill him. He had never thought that anyone would murder him, he was invulnerable: no one disliked him as much as that. On the other hand he knew that most people liked Linda more than they liked him. Even some of his friends grew to like her more than they liked him. He stared at his face in the window. It was thin and worried and the brows were corrugated as he had thought they might be. He leaned forward and studied his reflection more closely: why, it was like the face of an insane man, with the lips tighter and thinner than usual. He pulled away from the window as the reflections of the cows in the fields leaped into focus. At least, lying in the sun and chewing grass, they didn't have his problems.

He set off in search of Linda. She was standing by a door staring thoughtfully out at the landscape.

"Listen," he said urgently, "there's something that I want you to do for me and it will prove whether I can trust you or not." Of course, he said to himself, he didn't trust her whatever he said to her but at the same time he must be as cunning as she was, wear a mask. People wore masks all the time, no one could ever understand another person, no one could ever communicate with another person, that was an axiom inevitable and pure. "Listen," he said, "what I want you to do is this. When the train stops at the station I want you to go to the compartment where my case is and ask a porter to take the case from the rack and put it on his barrow, then wheel it to the gate where I will be waiting. I'm going to get off the train immediately it stops at Queen St in Glasgow. I shall wait for you at the gate where the ticket collectors are." That will confuse them, he thought. They are expecting me to go back for the case in person, and they will be waiting for me. But I won't go back for my case. Furthermore by this plan I am putting Linda in a quandary. Of course she is in alliance with these men but the beauty of her scheme is that she doesn't want me to know that she has betrayed me. She will pretend to the very end that she loves me; to do otherwise would be a failure of her scheme. Wouldn't it be splendid for her if he went to his grave without her having confirmed his suspicions of her treachery in any way? Wouldn't that be her final triumph?

So he watched her and the ripple of surprise that played like water about her face. Of course she was discomfited: he had checkmated her. In any case he played chess and she didn't. He wondered what she would say: it was as if her very brain was naked to his gaze and he could actually see its workings as clearly as the pistons which drove the train through the hills.

"I don't mind," she said at last. "But isn't that rather odd?"

"Not at all," he said. "I don't trust these two men. I'll go out first and then you get a porter to take the case to the gate. It's simple enough. And then I can trust you."

"All right," she said. "If that's what you want."

"That's what I want," he said.

She turned away from him to look out the window and he gazed with satisfaction at her back. Bitch, he had checkmated her that time. She couldn't get out of the trap he had set for her. On the other hand, when she went back to get the case, might she not tell the two men what had happened? It might be better if he stayed where he was so that he would see if she went back before they were about to arrive at the station. He had to think of everything, it was all very exhausting.

He imagined her mind squirming at this moment among the stones of her reality. She was trying to find a way out of her predicament such that he wouldn't be suspicious. But he couldn't become unsuspicious now, there was no way in which that could happen. Once the shadow fell across the peaceful unambiguous landscape you couldn't return it to its cage again. Innocence was a condition that one couldn't recapture once it had been lost.

He thought this out for a long time and knew that it was true. Never again would he be able to trust her. This was the elegy of their marriage. Before, he had trusted her, but everything had now changed. A terrible treachery had been born. He stared at her dumb back and could hardly believe that he and she had changed so much. But it had happened, and perhaps on a lesser scale it happened to everyone after a while. Marriage was to a certain extent an economic contract, wasn't it? Didn't the sociologists say that?

He moved back from the window to stand beside the open door of the compartment in which were sitting the man and woman whom he had talked to earlier. And at that moment he saw the hefty man walking towards him along the corridor, rolling from side to side because of the speed of the train. No, he couldn't do anything to him here, that was certain. Not in this corridor with the sunlight shining on it. So absorbed was he in his thoughts that he didn't at first realize that the hefty man had spoken to him. What had he asked him? Was there a buffet on this train? Of course there was no buffet on the train, there never had been a buffet on this train. Moreover the hefty man knew that there hadn't been. He had merely taken this excuse for speaking to him, while all the time smiling at him in a crooked knowing manner, as if he were implying, I know who you are, I know all your tricks, I know that you know who and what I am. Isn't this a tremendous game? But he himself didn't smile, no, he watched the hefty man returning down the corridor after he had discovered what he knew already. Damn him, damn him: why was he laughing at him so openly? He was the bully of his dreams, the one he had seen in his nightmares when he was still at school. That bully too had smiled in the same superior manner, that bully

26

too had looked confident and self-sufficient and strong: that bully too had been his master. And also just before the hefty man had turned away, he had looked at Linda, smiled and shaken his head. And she had shaken her head as well as if she and he were in a conspiracy together as of course they were.

At that very moment she was making as if to return to the compartment where his case was, but he thrust himself in her way.

"No," he said, "not yet." She stared at him despairingly and then asked faintly "Why not?"

"No reason," he said.

So, he turned back to the window again but not before a tall youth had looked at the two of them, about to say something but then deciding against it. Of course the youth thought he was bullying his wife: if only he knew!

Once he had written a story about Horatio left on his own after Hamlet's death. And Horatio sat in his corner in the new court in Denmark where all the trains now ran on time, where all the parks were a uniform antiseptic green, where crystal and glass glittered everywhere, and Fortinbras set out in his hunting boots and red coat every morning in search of the elusive cindery fox, and Horatio couldn't bring himself to speak, for the story was too complicated to tell. No one would believe him if he told what had happened and furthermore his audience was not the kind that he wanted. So he grew old and became a bore and then one day he left the castle, where there were now no secret curtains, and never came back. And Fortinbras too was glad of it for he was tired of Horatio's silence.

So it was with himself and Linda. He couldn't bring himself to tell people of her trick with the telephone book, for instance, and who would believe him? Certainly not that tall youth in the denim jacket, especially when he could look at her and see that her face was deceptively pale. But Ralph wouldn't let her past him till the last minute. He couldn't afford to allow her to tell the two men of his new plan. And so he stood there like a sentry, as if guarding her from harm, when all the time he was watching her closely.

The train bulleted on and he still stood there. And after a while he grew tired. To hell with it, he said to himself, let her go back. I'll go and sit down but this time I'll sit among a crowd of people in an open carriage. Surely I can't be harmed in such a place. He opened the door of the carriage and sat down heavily, feeling the tiredness in his very bones. He squeezed past two youths and sat at the window even though there were other vacant places he might have taken and which were more accessible. He stared dully out at the landscape which was flying past, aware that the two youths were watching him. But he didn't care. What he had to do was preserve his life, and mockery was a small price to pay.

'When You and I Were Young, Maggie', the train sang, and it was as if his head were a record spinning, a black disc revolving. The racing train was carrying him to Glasgow, city of green and blue, city of violent action: he didn't even know where he was going to stay. The important thing was to get into a taxi and ask the driver to take him to a hotel somewhere so that he could sleep. He must sleep, he hadn't slept for days, weeks. Linda complained that in the middle of the night he would waken her up and interrogate her. One morning he had wakened up and gone to type in his room, his head totally clear as if filled with moonlight. And then he had collapsed, exhausted on his bed.

He glanced at his watch. Shortly they would be pulling into Queen St station. Another fifteen minutes perhaps. He stared out the window and couldn't see the names of the stations, the train was going so fast. It was as if the driver sensed like a salmon his destination and was heading for it at breakneck speed. Maybe he wanted to get home for his tea. What an extraordinary thing, Ralph considered, no what an ordinary thing, that the driver should be thinking of his tea and he himself of his own death. A nostalgia for the ordinary almost engulfed him: it was so intense that it brought tears to his eyes.

And then another thought occurred to him. He was angry with himself that it had not occurred to him before. Just before one arrived at Queen St station the train passed through a tunnel and the carriages became black as pitch, so that even the pallor of a face could not be distinguished in the darkness. This happened just after they had made the stop near the tenements, one of which had a coloured mural on its ancient gable. On the walls one could see the scrawled slogans of the illiterate, the pitiful Glasgow adolescent gangs, in letters red as blood as if written by Dracula. Imagine how he had passed them in earlier days and hadn't taken them seriously. Why, they were only the pleas of the failed egos for attention, much as his own books were, according to Linda, they weren't to be considered or studied in any depth. Poor illiterate schoolboys, poor sorrowful aggressive lost souls, writing on the blackboards of stone, open to the wind and the rain and the pervasive dirt and dust.

He waited, and sure enough the darkness descended: no, 'descended' was the wrong word. It thickened around him, palpable, dense. He moved his neck forward in his seat. He was thinking that perhaps the hefty man would lean forward in the darkness having first marked his position, and then proceed to strangle or garotte him in a leisurely manner. The darkness was not a diminution of light but a complete absence of it, and yet a presence of its own too. An absence of light! What would happen if there was no light? There would be no poetry, no prose, no art at all, unless perhaps a totally new kind of literature and painting would emerge. Its kings would be those who walked in darkness, who loved the clouds and the lightless places. Stony statues with rain dripping down their carved skirts. Think of those early artists who had crawled through caves to stab at walls with their phantom weapons, which were really the weapons of art, creating the defenceless imagined animals.

And then like a huge blossom the light leaped around him, and he was there in his seat, safe, untouched. There was no sign of either the scarred man or the hefty man. There was no sign of Linda either. The train was drawing into the station. Very quickly he pushed past the two youths, pushed the window down, and opened the door. Quickly he ran towards the exit. He handed his ticket over to a ticket collector who seemed to have soup stains on his jacket, and then, crouching behind the barrier, watched. So far he could see neither of the two men nor Linda. And then he did. They were standing at the end of the train talking to her and she was shaking her head. Ralph watched closely as he saw the porter putting the case on his trolley. The two men walked slowly towards the exit. Ralph crouched down so that they could not see him, and then they were making their way into the hubbub of Glasgow, but not before he had seen the hefty man smile as if he had seen him.

But, no, they didn't wholly disappear. He could see them standing in the taxi queue. But that could wait. Linda was walking beside the porter who had the case on his trolley. He pushed it through the exit, she handed over her ticket, and then she was standing beside him. He seized the case and said to her, "We'd better wait for a while."

"What for?"

"No reason. I just want to wait for a while. Would you like a coffee?"

"No, thanks."

As a matter of fact he himself didn't want coffee either. He didn't like the buffet. There were too many tramps haunting it, violent unstable aggressive men with beards, and long coats falling to their ankles. Sometimes however a policeman would stroll through it, watching for trouble.

"All right then," he said, "we can go on." He carried the case, and Linda followed him obediently. He reached the Left Luggage and on an impulse said, "I think we'll leave the case here."

"Why?"

"I don't know. I just want to."

"If you like," said Linda indifferently. "But hadn't you better take your shaving gear out of it, and your pyjamas."

He knelt down and transferred the articles she had mentioned to her small red case. Then he handed his own case over and received a ticket in exchange. He put it carefully in his wallet, making sure that Linda didn't see the number on it. Why, she might tell the other two, if she knew the number.

When they had walked past the Gents and the Ladies he saw that the two men were no longer in the queue. On the other hand they might know certain taxi drivers who would watch out for himself and Linda. They might even have told Linda to watch out for one of them. He studied Linda closely to see if she was making a signal but she did nothing suspicious.

A taxi drew up and he and Linda got into it. Ralph leaned back as if he had been running a race: he was panting a little. The chatter of the driver's microphone bothered him: he thought that the driver might be receiving secret instructions. But he was determined that he would remain cool and unflustered.

"Ask him the name of a good hotel," he said to Linda.

He listened as if in a dream and heard the taxi driver mentioning some hotels on Sauchiehall St.

"Right," he said, "I'll choose the Stewart."

"Fine," said Linda, "do you know anything about it?"

"No, nothing, but it sounds as good as any."

"That's okay," said Linda. "I don't mind which you choose." Yet it seemed to him that he had been predestined to choose that particular hotel and that Linda had read his mind. But surely that could not be possible. As if by accident he touched her breast briefly, checking that she might not have a transmitter or some other method of sending a message. Maybe she had some means of keeping in touch with these two hoods, for he was sure that she had employed them. Glasgow was more than ever dangerous: in his imagination he saw it as a place of duels with knives and razors. He saw his own face striped with blood like a tiger's. He was trembling. He spread out his fingers in front of him and they were shaking as if with fever. Perhaps he should get rid of Linda now. Perhaps it had been a mistake to bring her with him. Maybe he should leap out of the taxi while it was standing at a red light and lose himself in the maze of the city.

In profile she looked innocent and as if carved from marble. She was often bloodless of course and sometimes took a tonic. The number of tonics he had bought for her, how solicitous he had been, and this was how she repaid him. Damn, damn, damn. No one would believe this story if he wrote it down. It was a thrilling novelettish lightweight sort of thing, it was a jigsaw narrative like Glasgow itself. He felt anger rising in him again after the long silence of his dismembered pages. Even now he could hardly believe that she was doing what she was doing. Of course it was her cleverness that had made her follow him, for otherwise she might have lost sight of him. He might have disappeared in Glasgow and taken his books and money with him. No, she had been quick-witted enough to realize that she must not lose sight of him. First of all, she had tried to persuade him to go back to the house but when that tactic had failed she had pretended to weep, and followed him to Glasgow.

The taxi drew up in front of a large hotel with a tartan frontage and tartan carpet in the foyer. It looked quite expensive, and in the middle of the foyer were exhibition cases with Doulton figures. He stopped at the desk as if marooned in a desert.

"Mr and Mrs Walton," he said before Linda could speak. That was clever of him, to think of changing his name. Linda was about to say something but only stared at him in a puzzled manner. "From Ayr," he wrote. No car, nationality British. A young man led them to the lift, and seemed harmless enough. Then they were climbing inside what seemed to him a large steel safe, and had been let out. The room was Number 520. The boy opened the door for them, Ralph handed him a 50p piece, and then he was in the room and shutting the door behind him. When he had done this he lay down on the bed while Linda took off her coat and hung it in the wardrobe. His eyes vaguely wandered around the room, from the telephone which lay on a small table beside the bed, to the ceiling decorated as if with icing, and then to the floor with its tartan carpet. He saw Linda's eyes noting the telephone, and said to himself, So that's it. If I leave you alone in this room you will phone your friends and they will come to the anonymity of a Glasgow hotel and kill me. After all no one knew now where he was, and he had even given a false name. They would probably remove all means of identification from his clothing.

As he watched Linda he was amazed to see how calm and cool she seemed. How could she possibly be so when she had been so deceitful, when she was determined to get rid of him, had in fact hired people to do so. She wanted him not to be able to prove that she was a traitor. But he would know. If these two men came in the middle of the night he would surely know. There would be one moment when he would know and that would be a satisfaction to him. It was like a story by John Dickson Carr or Ellery Queen, the solution would be revealed at the end, the villain would be unmasked, and all would at last be plain and radiant. He would at last understand what he had suspected but could not prove.

"I'll go to the bathroom," said Linda in the same unnaturally calm voice and he listened to her moving about in it. Then very quickly he rose and tiptoed over to the bathroom and looked in. Linda was on her knees beside the toilet bowl.

"What are you doing?" he asked in a loud voice.

She rose quickly to her feet, looking flustered.

"I . . . I dropped an earring," she said. "I was searching for it."

"No, you weren't," he said. "You were putting a bug in here. I know that's what you were doing." And he himself went down on his knees and tried to find the bug but he couldn't locate it though he knew it was there. He didn't know much about bugs but had an idea that it could be disguised as perhaps the head of a nail: but there were so many of these that there was no point in even beginning to look. She might even have put the bug behind the large blank mirror that took up most of one side of the bathroom. He was more than ever convinced that she was deceiving him and that she recorded everything he said, to bring it up later as evidence of his unreasonableness and his manic tendencies. "He was always looking for bugs," she would say, "isn't that in itself evidence of his madness?" The clarity of his own mind was intense. It was as if he could see and hear right across counties, countries, even Europe. He had never before had such piercing clarity and ease of understanding. But he had to be quick and intelligent, for he was fighting for his life.

"Please," he said to Linda. "Why don't you stop it? You know that I loved you in the past. I never meant you any harm."

"What are you talking about," she said.

"What I said. Why do you hate me so much?"

"It's you who hate me," she said. "I don't hate you. You should go to sleep. Why don't you take a pill?"

"No," he said, "I won't."

He was determined that he wouldn't take a sleeping tablet for he was sure that in his stupor of sleep she would phone her two friends and let them in and then they would kill him. He tried to remember whether they had been given a choice of rooms and couldn't. Had she for some reason of her own chosen this room?

He went over to the window. Far below he could see cars like toys and people like dolls walking along the pavements. There was a huge glass building opposite the hotel but he didn't know what it was. He shuddered and shut the window.

"I still think you should sleep for a while," said Linda, "and maybe later we can go down for dinner."

"You sleep if you want," he said, "but I'm staying awake."

"All right then," she said. "I'll lie down for a while." She removed her shoes and lay on the bed. It occurred to him that if she thought he was mad she should be more afraid of him. Damn you, he said, you threw a glass of whisky in my face once at a publisher's party. And then he was analysing memories of past quarrels. Sometimes she would read the Bible to him, as if it was a sword she was placing between herself and him, a shield, naked

33

and virginal. At times she had been frightened of him as if he were driving her crazy.

"No," he would shout. "It was you who twisted my mind. You take everything I say so seriously and you are always looking for slights. I've never seen anyone as sensitive as you."

"But that's because of you and your friends," she would say. "You are all so cold and calculating and egotistic. I never see slights that aren't there."

As he saw her lying on the bed, his own mind preternaturally active, he tried to work out where she had her bug. It might be in her handbag which was always cluttered with stuff: on the other hand she might have it somewhere on her body. Maybe that night as they lay in bed together the microphone would pick up his very breathing. He would have to be very careful what he said to her for she was infinitely cunning. And then tapes could be cut and spliced and their sense and content changed completely, and what was most incriminating preserved.

His head nodded on his chest and he thought that he would soon fall asleep, and yet he mustn't do that. He rose and went to the bathroom and splashed cold water over his face, and then very quickly returned again. By this time Linda seemed to him to be lying nearer the telephone, as if she had wakened up, and then sensing him coming back had pretended to go to sleep again. He must watch her, he must not sleep.

Oh God, how closely we are tied together, he thought. We are inseparable. On the other hand, if she hadn't insisted on coming with him he would now have been sleeping peacefully. Or he might be sitting up in bed reading a book, perfectly relaxed, perhaps even smoking a cigarette. But he couldn't sleep as long as she was there. Her eyes were closed, her breast rose and fell gently, he could see the watch and bracelet on her hand which was thrown limply across the bed. How vulnerable she looked, how cunning.

Suddenly he remembered that she had brought with her the machine which she used for slimming. She usually tied a belt around her waist and the machine vibrated gently. He sought in her handbag and found it. That was it, the slimming machine was where the bug was, he was sure of that now. Why else had she taken it with her? He took it over to the window, she still asleep and breathing serenely, and violently tugged and tugged at it till he broke it. Then he threw the mangled fragments into the waste-paper basket and sat down in his chair again.

Maybe he should write a message on a piece of paper and throw it down to the street so that people would know what was happening to him. On the other hand there was so much litter in Glasgow that people might not notice it. He had liked Glasgow in the past — after all he had lived there fifty years ago — but now he was afraid of it. He felt it as an alien frightening presence. Sometimes he would see tramps on the street, in the buffet at the railway station, with their long greasy coats, and they disturbed him. Maybe he himself would become like them some day. The number of people in the city depressed him, there was no privacy. Clocks were always stopped. Men and women at newspaper stands clapped their hands in the cold like cockerels clapping their chilly wings. Youths with orange or green or red hair, spikily arranged like thorns, patrolled the streets.

He could no longer hear the traffic since he had shut the window. Linda's breath was calm and rhythmical. Her face was pale and there were blue shadows under her eyes like faint bruises. Her pure white blouse was spotless and she was wearing her amethyst brooch, the one he had given her for her birthday. How much did he really know about her? Oh, he knew a lot about her superficially, she had earned her living as a secretary, but what else did he know about her? Nothing really. What went on inside her head? Though they were nearly the same age, she seemed somehow to be younger than him: she thought of him as an old fogey. She might want to marry someone else, someone less absorbed in his work. How had they driven down different roads, how had their minds diverged from each other and gone down separate paths? Perhaps all marriages were like that. And yet he was convinced that he had made more compromises than she had. Why, he had learned even to talk to her when what he most wanted at the time was to read or write. Couldn't she see the sacrifice he had made there? But, no. All that he had done for her, but what had she done for him? Well, yes, she had allowed him his days of silence at the desk, had even bought the desk for him and the filing cabinet. He had to admit that.

She was now lying awake on her bed and gazing at him with direct eyes.

"Look," she said, "are you feeling all right? You look awfully flushed."

"I'm fine," he said.

"I'm not so sure about that. You had better watch your heart. Why don't you lie down?"

"No, thanks. I'm fine, I tell you."

"Do you remember," she said, "that tune you used to like so much. 'When You and I Were Young Maggie'. It came into my head just now."

"What?" he said.

"It just came into my head. Out of nowhere."

So that was it. She was determined to drive him mad. How else could she have known that he heard that tune on the train? She must have some method of getting inside his mind, she must be directing his mind like a conductor of an orchestra. She had probably directed him to this hotel as well.

"I never understood why you liked that tune so much," she said sleepily. And she began to hum it.

"Stop it," he said, suddenly and angrily. "Please stop it. I don't want to hear that tune. I've turned against it."

"What about 'Irene Good Night' then. That was another of your favourites. You've nothing against that one, have you?"

He gazed at her helplessly. Oh, she was so subtle, there was nothing that she wasn't able to do. Women were much more subtle than men. In comparison with women men were simply overgrown boys.

"I'd prefer it if you didn't hum at all," he said. "I really would. Why don't you go back to sleep?"

"I don't feel sleepy now," she replied. "Not at all."

"Neither do I."

"Well, then," she said, "why don't we go down for dinner. I'm sure it must be near dinner-time now. Do you want me to phone and ask them?"

"No," he said. "We'll go down."

"I had better go to the bathroom and freshen up then," she said.

"All right, I'll come with you."

"I beg your pardon?"

"I'll come with you. What's wrong with that?"

"Well, it's not exactly . . ." She shrugged her shoulders. "Still, if you feel you must."

As she was just going into the bathroom she turned to him and said, "I try not to let it bother me, but I must say that all this is beginning to bug me."

Eventually they walked down the tartan-carpeted stair together. The dining-room was huge and cavernous with only two people in it, sitting at a table near the wall. They sat in silence for a while till a young boy wearing a white jacket came over to serve them. When he had gone the silence descended again.

"When are you going back?" said Ralph at last.

"I don't know. Do you want me to go back?"

"You can go back if you like."

In the old days Linda might have run crying out of the room, but now she sat there white and glacial.

"It hasn't worked out," said Ralph.

"No."

"It wasn't my fault. You shouldn't have torn the telephone book."

"For the last time I didn't touch it. Do you really think I would have torn your telephone book? What an extraordinary thing to do."

"Well, who else tore it? I didn't, that's for sure. And who mixed up the pages of my novel?"

"I don't know," said Linda.

He pecked at his food uninterestedly and so did Linda. They weren't really hungry though they had ordered dinner. He put his hand in his pocket and popped a pill in his mouth.

"Are you sure you should be taking these pills like sweets?" she said.

"I need them," he answered shortly.

The waiter was standing at the far end of the room staring at them. Maybe he was thinking of interfering, protecting Linda from him. He thought he had seen him before somewhere but that surely was not possible.

He passed his hand across his eyes. The people at the next table were laughing and shouting as before: it occurred to him that they too were in the plot, that they had been placed there in order to watch him.

And then quite suddenly they were gone as if they had never been. And he and Linda were alone again.

"What happened there?" he asked Linda.

"Where?"

"These people. They were there a minute ago and now they're gone."

"Maybe they didn't want to wait. Or perhaps they didn't like the menu."

"Hm."

Such strange things were happening around him. It was as if they had come to observe him and had left when they had done so.

"It's all very odd," he muttered.

"Are you sure you're all right?" said Linda looking at him keenly.

"Of course I'm all right. Why shouldn't I be all right?"

"It's just that . . ."

He felt so tired as if his mind couldn't absorb anything else.

"We'll have a bottle of wine," he said decisively.

"Are you sure?"

"Of course I'm sure."

He signalled the waiter over and ordered a bottle of Burgundy.

"Not Yugoslav wine?" she said.

"No," he said, knowing what she meant. He leaned towards her and caressed her cheek.

"What was that for?"

"The Last Supper," he said. "The betrayal. I know that you're carrying a bug and that everything I'm saying is being recorded."

"Your health," he said, ironically raising his glass to his lips.

"Cheers," she said.

The last time they had been at a party together she had had a long argument with a scholar and with her quick-wittedness had made him appear clumsy and ponderous. And then quite suddenly she had danced with the life that was in her, far more life than he had. Of course he was a Capricorn, remote, ambitious, cold. She on the contrary loved hospitality, wine and food.

But tonight she had left most of her prawn cocktail, and he was sure that she would leave most of her fish when it came, which it was doing now. The waiter bent towards them, servile, white-coated. This place was a trap, a draughty cave, empty and huge. Perhaps it was not a hotel at all, perhaps it was some other kind of building which had been selected for him. In the middle of the night she might take her red case and leave him there. He would have to be vigilant, stay awake, though he didn't feel like doing so. He drank another glass of the wine defiantly. It looked like blood. Never before had he seen it so clearly and blatantly as blood. He was like a vampire sucking his own blood. He put the glass of wine down on the table quickly spilling some of it, his hands shaking. The waiter looked at him briefly as he spooned the last of the fish on to the plate, and then turned away. One thing, he thought, there had been no Service Charge or Vat on the Last Supper. He smiled to himself: there was no point in telling Linda his joke for she would consider it blasphemy. Odd how religious she was in her own way, far more religious than him.

"Look," he said, "let's have peace between us. If you leave me alone I'll not write anything about you. I swear I won't."

"What do you mean, leave you alone?"

"What I said."

Linda sighed heavily and put her fish on one side. "I don't understand what you're talking about."

So she wasn't taking his offer of peace. Well then, let the sequel be on her own head. The room was swaying in front of him, the floor was rising and falling as if it was a high sea. The waiter was still standing at the far end of the cave staring at him. White coat, white coat . . .

And what had happened to the door? He couldn't see it. He searched around for it but it seemed to him that he was locked in and that Linda was laughing at him. Her face enlarged itself as in a fairground mirror.

"I think we should go upstairs," she said.

She placed her shawl across her shoulders and he followed her. There was a door after all; it seemed to have appeared out of nowhere. The lounge to his right was vaster than the dining-room and there was a TV set playing. The faces elongated and shortened and for a terrible moment he saw his own face on the screen and his own hand gesturing, pale and ghostly against a background of Renaissance reds.

"Listen," he said to Linda, but she had already gone ahead of him and was climbing the stairs.

He staggered after her. She seemed to be floating ahead of him and then she was fumbling at the door with her key. He decided not to go into the room, but turned away abruptly. He walked back along the corridor and came to the stair and descended. He passed door after door which he did not recognize and he knew that he was in hell. He spiralled downwards but he wasn't finding an entrance into the foyer at all. At the third turning of the second stair. . . . There were no windows anywhere and he couldn't see out and the stairs descended forever, perhaps to a boiler room. He knelt down on the stair and wept and then began to climb slowly again. There was no way out of the hotel. He was locked in and perhaps at this moment she was phoning to her two friends. Somehow or another she had manoeuvred him to this vain journey by reading his mind.

He ascended the stair unsteadily and found the corridor again. He walked past a number of doors, though the numbers on them seemed to have changed, and knocked on the door of his own bedroom.

"Let me in," he shouted urgently.

She opened the door and asked, "Where have you been?"

"Nowhere," he said. "I went down the stairs."

"What for?"

"No reason. I wanted to get out."

She hadn't been phoning after all: or perhaps she had been doing so while he was descending the stair into hell. She always looked so innocent. He locked the door, thinking despairingly that these two men might have skeleton keys.

"I think you should go to sleep," she said. "You look tired."

"No," he replied. "I must stay awake. But I will lie down."

"And take your clothes off," she said.

"All right," he said. "What did you do with the receipt for my case?"

"You've got it. You put it in your wallet."

He took out his wallet and searched for it. Sure enough there it was. He put his wallet under the pillow for safe keeping. He didn't want her to rise in the middle of the night and take out the case with his manuscripts and perhaps throw it into the Clyde.

The receipt was the most important thing in the universe for him at that moment. He removed his clothes and lay under the quilt. Before he did so he walked over to the window and stared down at the street again, so far below him. Lights were flickering and fluttering everywhere and tiny figures of people walked along the pavements. He was so high above . . . had she chosen that room for that very reason? The fifth floor, that was very high.

I must not sleep, he told himself over and over again. I must not sleep whatever happens. Linda had removed her clothes as well. She looked so beautiful, her hair so compact and fine. What a pity it was, what a terrible pity!

She snuggled into him and laid her head on his shoulders. He eased it away from him and lay flat on his back gazing at the ceiling. He put his hand under the pillow and withdrew his wallet, checking that his receipt was still there. In the middle of the night if he fell asleep she would take it away, he knew that. And then there would be no evidence that he had been to Glasgow at all.

He sighed. He could try and hide the receipt but there didn't seem to be any place where he could put it. She would watch him and know perfectly well where he had placed it.

He said, "So that's why you chose the fifth floor."

"What are you saying?"

You would. . . . He couldn't bring himself to say that she would with her two friends push him out of the window so that his body would splatter like a red star on the pavement below. Everyone of course would think that he had committed suicide. All his actions pointed to that, madness and suicide, he had been inveigled into participating in his own death. But he would have preferred any death to this one, a plunge like a wounded bird on to stone. Pills, a knife, poison, any of these he would have preferred, but she knew that he hated heights. That was why she had brought him to this last rendezvous. And furthermore he would never know that she had betrayed him.

"Why don't you tell me the truth?" he said. "Have pity. Tell me the plot, tell me you hate me." But she stared at him innocently. How clear and pure and loving her eyes seemed. So she wasn't even going to give him that satisfaction before he died. Damn her, damn her, damn her.

He felt his body plummeting down as he hit the stone. Curiously enough, he didn't care. He waited for events to happen as if they were inevitable, predestined. He was like a rabbit before the stoat's sinuous dance, and it didn't bother him any longer, not in the slightest. He had come to the end of the road, he was tired of thinking, of losing himself in these mazes without solution.

41

Let them kill him if they wanted to, he could no longer control the labyrinth of thoughts that tormented his mind.

"Shall I put the light off?" said Linda.

"If you like," he said.

She put the light out and he stared into the darkness and at the shadowy chair over which his trousers hung, at the shadowy wardrobe.

Linda tried again to put her head on his shoulder but he pushed her away. He knew that the bug was inside her dress but he didn't care: he was so tired. He felt very sleepy: he tried to keep his eyes open for he knew that he must. After all if those two men came in it would be in the early hours of the morning. He imagined the whole empty hotel with no one in it but himself and Linda: he saw again the huge abandoned foyer with the tartan carpet on the floor. He rubbed his eyes and felt dizzy.

"I think you should go to sleep," said Linda.

"Yes," he said, screwing his eyes against the darkness which was as heavy as a fleece.

"Well, let go," she said softly. "Nothing will happen to you."

"So you say," he mumbled.

No, he couldn't keep his eyes open. He must sleep. He couldn't even hear the traffic on the road below.

He slept.

It didn't seem long before he was awake again. Linda was shaking him by the shoulder and the light was on. There was a black man in the room, jingling keys in his pocket. The man's face was polished and bright and ebony. Surely this is hell, thought Ralph, this must be it at last. It was the devil he was looking at and the devil was smiling at him, so kindly. Linda was speaking.

"I sent for a doctor for you," she said. "I couldn't get to sleep. I was worried."

"What, what?" he said dazedly.

"This is a doctor here," said Linda, indicating the black man.

A doctor, the final doctor, the devil himself.

"You," he said, "you're not a doctor. What are you doing here? What's your name?"

And amazingly the man said, "Dr Emmanuel."

Ralph burst out laughing and could hardly stop.

"Who's to believe that?" he said. Dr Emmanuel, and he

42

laughed again hysterically. Linda was trying to drive him to the very limits of his sanity.

The devil looked meaningfully at Linda: his skin appeared almost purple in the light.

"Psychiatric treatment," he muttered. His tie was red and he was wearing a black shirt.

Oh, how well the devil had been coached. He even knew the word 'psychiatric'. He was trying to smile at Ralph but his smile was like a grimace, a wound.

Linda was saying, "Can't you take him to hospital then?"

So that was it then. She would place him in an asylum in the middle of slummy Glasgow and leave him there and go back home. He would never be heard of again. She would have him signed into some huge draughty ward where old men gibbered and spat and he would scream into a void.

"No, no," said the black man. "Can't take him to hospital here."

And Ralph was sure that he wasn't a doctor at all. This was a disguised man. The two terms — Emmanuel and negro — trembled together in his mind. He couldn't imagine that this was other than a bizarre joke, a scene in a play.

Linda was insistent. "Are you sure you can't put him in hospital?" she said.

"Am sure," said the doctor in broken English staring at Ralph as if he were a slide or a germ. "Psychiatric," he repeated, "not medical."

Linda went over to the phone. "Can you get me an outside line," she said.

She asked for Ralph's own doctor and eventually he heard her speaking to him, but of course it might not be his own doctor at all, it might be someone pretending to be him.

"Very ill. Yes, another doctor here." She put the black doctor on the line and Ralph heard as if from a great distance his own doctor speaking to the black doctor but then of course it might all be a charade. Then the black doctor ceased speaking and he heard Linda saying, "Are you sure? I'd better get back then."

"He wants to speak to you," said Linda.

Ralph picked up the phone and heard as if from a great hollow distance a voice saying to him,

"What's happening to you? It must be the Muse again." The

43

voice was jovial and it seemed to him false. The man at the other end of the phone laughed. Ralph considered that the voice might be coming from some part of the cavernous hotel itself: some ingenious arrangement had been set up, he didn't really believe it was his own doctor who sounded so flippant yet remote at the same time. He put the phone down impatiently and looked at the black man and Linda who were whispering together but immediately ceased when he put the phone down.

"Give him a sedative," said the black man to Linda. "To make him sleep." Linda nodded approvingly.

But Ralph didn't care. If they wanted to take him secretly from the hotel in the middle of the night while he was asleep, and confine him in an asylum, that was all right with him. Perhaps this hotel itself was an asylum. Maybe Linda had changed her plans. Throwing him out of the window was too risky, there would be questions asked. But if she made him totally disappear. . . . After all, that was what he had intended doing in the first place and she could simply say when she arrived home that he had run away from her in Glasgow. The doctor handed him two white pills and a glass of water. He swallowed the pills and drank the water and then saw the doctor taking his case which was lying on a chair.

"I didn't know," said Linda, "that you couldn't deal with him here."

"Own doctor," said the black man. And then, "Not possible."

Then he was gone as if he had been a genie from a bottle who had returned to it again in a smoky darkness. There was silence in the room and then Linda said, "He says you have to go back to your own doctor, that he can't treat you here."

"What did he say about me?" said Ralph, not believing that he was being told the truth. At first Linda didn't seem to hear him and then he repeated the question and she said, "Paranoid. He said you were paranoid. He said you needed psychiatric treatment."

How cunning she was. He hadn't heard the so-called doctor saying that at all. Now she wanted to get him home to that house where he had thought he was dying. His eyes felt heavy again and he tried to keep them open. They might come back in the middle of the night and take him to an asylum when he was asleep. But he didn't care. He felt so tired that he was willing to accept whatever destiny had prepared for him on the road on which he was travelling. The black doctor had been the ultimate brilliance of their plot, it was he who had finally made him realize that resistance was impossible, that his case was hopeless. And how clever they really were he hadn't known until now. How had he not appreciated the venom and cunning of the ordinary before: he had been cruising in the sky of his own high concerns without studying that world properly. Well, yes, in Yugoslavia he had seen it but he hadn't been fully aware of the folds and intricacies of it. How smart he had thought himself, how distant and intellectual, and yet he had been so easily deceived, as if he were a child. He had been the clumsy albatross who couldn't unfurl its wings from the bitter mediocrity of the ordinary. His eyes closed and he slept.

When he woke again it was broad daylight, which was pouring through the window, in which all objects were defined. He did not feel at all tired. On the contrary he felt that he could run out of the hotel and walk for miles in the sparkling air. His eyes lighted on a case which was lying on the floor and he thought that it must be some addition to the furniture of the hotel: he couldn't remember seeing it the night before. His eyes focussed on it and then he realized it was the case with his manuscripts which had been left in the Left Luggage. Linda was standing at the door as if expecting someone. She looked quite fresh and was dressed in her red velvet suit with the blue brooch at the breast. It was the amethyst brooch he had bought her at her last birthday.

"I took a taxi and collected the case in the middle of the night," she said.

"Did you open it?" he asked.

"No, it will be all right," she said.

"Where's the receipt?" he said looking for his wallet.

"I took it when you were asleep," she said. "I'll open it if you like."

She opened the case and it seemed to him that his manuscripts were undisturbed. On the other hand, could he remember exactly which manuscripts had been in it?

He found it very hard to concentrate.

"I think they will be all right," said Linda, closing the case again. "I sent for some breakfast." She glanced at the slender gold watch on her wrist. "It should be coming any moment now. And I've ordered a taxi to take us home."

"A taxi?" he said.

"Yes," she said. "There's no train on a Sunday. You remember that, don't you?"

"Yes," he said. "But a taxi!" It must be a hundred miles to go home.

On the other hand it might be that she wasn't taking him home at all, it might be that she was taking him to a different part of Glasgow. He would have to keep a close watch. He felt sweaty again and rose and splashed water from the basin all over his chest. As soon as he had done so Linda packed his pyjama jacket, which he had removed, in his case. She looked quite cool and competent though she could hardly have had any sleep.

"Do you remember the black doctor who was here?" she said.

"I remember a black man," he answered.

At that moment a waiter came in with a trolley on which there was some breakfast.

"I asked for porridge for you," said Linda. "And scrambled eggs." She placed the tray on the bed and he poured cream on to the porridge and then thought of something. "You take some of this first," he said.

"All right," said Linda. "Did you think I was poisoning you?" She ate some of the porridge and only then did he eat it though he was hungry.

It appeared to him now that he was safe from the windows, one of which was open. The curtain fluttered in the early fresh breeze of the morning. How lovely and airy and vernal everything suddenly seemed, washed clear of plot and counterplot. Why, even Linda seemed new and uncorrupted in her red velvet costume as if there was nothing at all on her mind. He ate his porridge and his scrambled egg and Linda said, "You should get dressed now. The taxi won't be long. I've been down at the desk and paid the bill for the hotel." What a busy little bee she must have been, flitting now here now there in the middle of the night as he himself lay asleep. Why, he hadn't even heard her removing the wallet from below his pillow. How unprotected and vulnerable he must have been! But how did all this fit into the plot? She must have abandoned the first one and devised a new one. Oh, he could hardly keep up with her, her manoeuvrings and subtleties. All this he thought while he was dressing and at the same time feeling so fresh that he could see through any plot or plan or conspiracy that anyone could devise.

"Is this the same room we were in during the night?" he asked.

"Of course. What made you think it was different?"

"I don't know. Was that chest there last night?" And he pointed.

"Of course it was."

"Oh."

He went into the bathroom and shaved. His face looked pale, intent, and thin, and his eyes heavy. He leaned forward towards the mirror, sensing that his face had somehow changed. It looked like that of a monkey again, small and withered and clenched. Why, I'm changing, he said to himself, and he felt intense panic again. When he had shaved he sat on the bed and waited. Linda was still standing at the door but he was not afraid now. She couldn't do anything to him in the sunlight which poured in a healthy and almost holy radiance around him. Daylight was the time of innocence, night the time of guilt. And the night had passed, the worst night of his life, infernal and terrible, had passed. He hoped that no night like that would ever descend on him again.

"Did you know," he said to Linda. "I tried to get out of the hotel last night but I couldn't. There were no doors leading from the stairs."

"That's not true," she said. "There are doors leading from the stairs. You saw them yourself when we came up in the lift."

"Lift?" he said.

"Yes, we came up in the lift. Don't you remember?"

No, he couldn't remember.

"And there was a TV set. In the lounge," he said.

"I never noticed it," said Linda carelessly.

"And I saw my face in it," said Ralph. "It looked Japanese."

"I'm sorry I didn't notice."

He shook and perspired again and the floor and walls were leaving him, going off to another country. Sometimes he could see Linda, quite normal and harmless as he had always seen her up to now, and at other times he saw her as evil, sinuous, snakelike. He couldn't understand how she looked so rested. She wasn't trembling as he was. But, no, she didn't look at all frightened. And yet she should be. What if he turned on her, what if he himself tried to throw her out of the window, so great was his hate for her. It surprised him that she wasn't more scared of him if

47

she considered him mad. But no, he was not mad, it was simply that the world had become more clear to him, that appearances which he had accepted quite simply, had now become enormously complicated. He had become the visionary which all ordinary people already were. He had made the ascent to the ordinary and found it more snakelike than the extraordinary. But that was how ordinary people had to live, wasn't it? They fought each other for air; like flowers in the darkness of the earth they had to maintain constant control over each other, they could not ignore any attempt on their freedom. But how else could ordinary people live, without art, without an obsession?

He considered this for a long time. It seemed to him that door after door was opening and that they revealed avenues and corridors of light, blazing and contemptuous. Of course they must all live like that since there was no alternative. They must not allow each other more than the permitted space since otherwise they would be at a disadvantage. The world of the ordinary was strange to him, like another country whose language he could not understand but which ordinary people could articulate at once because of the gift that they had. They were determined to pull him down from the height of his talent to the slummy maze of their lives. Every word people spoke was coded and loaded with significance since each might be a disguised attack. Far more to them than to him was language significant: that was what he hadn't understood. Slights, insults, they were the experts on that form of language, it was the undergrowth of their shrunken venomous minds.

There was a knock on the door and a man entered. It was another waiter, this time dressed in a black suit.

"The taxi, madam," he said.

"Come on," said Linda. He picked up the case with his manuscripts while she carried her own small red case. He cast a last look around the room. Never again would he see it, never again would he sleep in it. And it was like leaving a safe haven, for the end of the plot was not yet in sight. They walked down the stairs together and he could see now the entrances to the corridors and to the foyer. It was as if the hotel had been changed physically during the night like a stage-set that revolved in a void. Linda walked briskly ahead of him and they were in the foyer while, outside, the taxi was waiting.

The tartan-carpeted floor stretched in front of him and around him in all directions. There were other guests at the desk paying for their rooms before leaving. How had he not seen them the night before? From what hidden chambers had they been disgorged into the ordinary daylight? And the girl at the desk too looked ordinary, as if she were a real receptionist in a real hotel.

The taxi driver was a calm affable man: but Ralph of course knew that he was not a taxi driver at all. Nor was his taxi a real taxi, though it had been made up to look like one. Taxis reminded him of hearses anyway, black and closed. However he climbed into it, bumping his head on the top of the door as he did so, and sat in the back seat, Linda clambering in after him. He was determined to remain silent, on whatever journey they were taking him.

And then the thought occurred to him. This so-called taxi driver was really Linda's lover, the one she met when she was away from home. The more he thought about this the more he was sure of its truth. Why else had she asked for a taxi when it would cost a fortune to go back to the village in it? He was the sort of big man that he was certain she secretly admired. He was in fact quite extraordinarily big, big enough to control Ralph, and perhaps hustle him into a secret asylum on this secret route they would take. He would have to watch him very carefully.

Linda and the taxi driver were now talking banalities, she of course pretending that she didn't know him. They were talking about the demolition of Glasgow and the way it had changed.

"I used to be frightened of Glasgow," said Linda, "but not now. It was full of dirty tenements."

"That's right," said the taxi driver. "Do you see how they have been cleaning the faces of the buildings, sandblasting them." And, sure enough, they did look cleaner than he remembered.

"They say Glasgow is very violent," said Linda. "Not that I ever saw any myself."

"I haven't seen much either," said the taxi driver.

She asked him questions about whether he was frightened at night with some of the customers that he got. But, no, he wasn't, though some were drunk and refused to pay.

It turned out that he was Catholic, and had six children.

"My wife's got three fur coats," he said. "Not that I'm bragging. She's a nurse."

49

All the way along the road, Linda was desperately talking and all the way Ralph was scrutinizing the route to see if the taxi driver was indeed taking him back to the village. Once or twice he thought of opening the door and jumping out: that would be better than remaining for the rest of his life in an asylum among mad violent people, when he himself was perfectly sane. He imagined himself making a faint dying arc from the taxi on to the blurred road, but he didn't have the nerve for the ultimate jump. It was also important to him to see the end of the plot, to watch Linda revealing herself as the villainness she was.

The taxi driver didn't speak to Ralph and Ralph didn't speak to him. It was as if Linda and the driver were trying to cover his silence by their boring conversation which ran like a river around him.

"I once took a lady around the country to the north of Scotland," said the driver. "She needed a chauffeur. We spent a week touring. She had tons of money. An old lady too, a small woman with grey hair. She was home on a holiday from Canada."

"Oh," said Linda.

"She was always stopping to go to the toilet," said the taxi driver. "There was something wrong with her kidneys."

"Isn't that odd," thought Ralph, "that's exactly what Linda's mother was like when we were in . . ." But he couldn't even say the name of the country to himself, he had hated it so much.

And then because the taxi driver's wife was a nurse, Linda began to talk about hospitals and a nurse she had known. This nurse had told her that the old people in the geriatric hospital had called her by different names so that by the end of the day she didn't know who she was. And then there was an old lady who believed that she was pregnant and who was waiting for her husband to come and visit her with a bouquet of flowers (what she had actually said was a "banquet" of flowers. This old lady was always misusing words). And then another old woman had told her that she had come into the ward one day to find sick men in pyjamas lying all over the place.

"She must have gone into the men's ward by mistake," said the taxi driver.

"She might have done. Only she thought they were Americans who had mistaken the hospital for a hotel and they were all lying there in their silk pyjamas."

The taxi driver laughed, and Ralph thought, By talking about incidents like this they are trying to disorientate me. But I will not be disoriented. I have my identity and I will keep it. That story about having six children was obviously untrue. He probably wasn't married at all. Even a child could see through their machinations.

When they arrived in the village, what he would have to do was, ask the taxi driver to take him in to see his own doctor and according to how he reacted to that suggestion he would know whether he was genuine or not. He wanted to see his own doctor anyway and get tablets from him.

The road unwound like a lost white ribbon, the taxi driver and Linda talked on. They had now left Glasgow and were heading north. If he was going to be put in an asylum it wouldn't be in Glasgow, that was for sure. The Sunday morning was quiet and cool and there were few cars on the road. He lay back in his corner seat and closed his eyes, trying to keep away from Linda, withdrawing when the lurch of the taxi threw them occasionally together.

As a matter of fact he didn't want to talk anyway. It was as if the power of speech had left him, as if he had sunk into the most profound lassitude and darkness. He focussed his eyes on the broad back of the taxi driver and thought, If only I were like him then Linda would not have considered leaving me. How competent he was, how effortlessly and expertly he drove. This taxi driver had probably learned to drive quite easily, had never had any trouble with practical matters. Why was it that there were some men who had this innate competence while others had to work so hard at everything they did. On the other hand writing was a gift which he himself had, his talent in that was assured and clear without the shadow of a doubt lying on it.

"I would like to go on to the town of . . . to see my doctor," he said aloud in a firm voice.

It seemed to him that the taxi driver glanced at Linda in his mirror and winked at her.

"I would like to go on and see my doctor," he repeated.

"But the surgery won't be open on a Sunday," said Linda.

"It doesn't matter. We can go to his house. After all, I'm paying for this taxi."

The taxi driver remained silent, waiting for Linda to speak.

She said again, "I don't think the doctor would be very pleased. He can call tomorrow. What you need is a good rest."

"I want to see the doctor," he repeated. "The fact is I don't think this is a real taxi. It would make me happier if I saw my doctor."

"You don't really want to see your doctor," said the taxi driver, as if he were talking to a child. "As your wife says, the doctor's surgery will be shut today."

"It's none of your business," said Ralph angrily.

"I'm not afraid of you," thought Ralph to himself angrily. "You may be big and strong and my wife's lover but I'm not frightened of you."

They were now out in the country: land stretched away on both sides of them with sheep feeding on the grass. There was the sudden glitter of a loch: and a house with a slanted roof like the house of a witch. For a moment Ralph imagined that there was a woman leaning out of the attic window, like Mrs Rochester plotting her fire. He often invented fantasies like this when he was travelling. But then hadn't he come to a dead stop with his novel? For days he had sat and stared at the white empty page unable to continue.

"I will not go mad," he kept saying to himself. "I will not go mad. I am not mad. This is a plot aimed at me. I am perfectly sane. There was never any madness in my family. There was coldness, remoteness, but there was never any madness." The sheep grazed contentedly and the fields were intersected with rays of yellow light.

"Sweet day so clear so calm so bright,
    the bridal of the earth and sky," he repeated silently to himself. Usually he hated Sundays which seemed to last forever. But now he was frightened.

"Look," he said coldly and aloud to Linda, "I know you for what you are." She woke up in a startled manner and stared at him.

"Sir," said the taxi driver, politely and protectively.

"You keep out of it," said Ralph fiercely.

"It doesn't matter," said Linda. "Let him carry on."

"I know you for what you are," said Ralph savagely. "I remember the time you danced with that small bald man at the party and you created when I danced with the blonde girl."

"That was a long time ago," said Linda. "And anyway I can't remember."

The large hands of the taxi driver rested on the wheel but he didn't speak, though Ralph could tell that he was listening intently. That bloody pseudo-Catholic from some nameless Glasgow housing scheme.

The landscape outside the window shimmered. He remembered an incident that had happened not so long before he had run away. Linda had been working in the kitchen and he himself had been typing in his room. Suddenly he had seen a girl in a leather coat, carrying a carton of milk, walk across the gravel in the direction of the kitchen door. She hadn't looked in through the window where he himself was typing and after a while he had seen her returning and going out by the gate. Later, when he and Linda were having coffee, he had asked her who the girl was.

"What girl?" Linda had said.

"A girl in a leather coat. She was carrying a carton of milk."

"That's odd," Linda had said. "I never saw such a girl." And then she had tried to pass the incident off lightly by saying, "You must have been thinking of one of your girl friends." And indeed she had looked like Irma. He had dismissed the incident from his mind but now and again it would return to him and he would shake his head in a puzzled manner. Was it true that he had imagined the girl or had Linda simply denied her existence for some deep reason of her own? Had she asked the girl to call and then deliberately insisted that she didn't exist? How much, he thought, we rely for our sanity on witnesses without prejudice. Without them we would be gnashing our teeth in the outer darkness.

Another twenty miles or so and then he would be home. The house would appear out of its familiar space with its garden and its cherry tree. The taxi would stop and he and Linda would get out and then the taxi driver would drive away, still pretending that he was a real taxi driver. And then he might phone Linda and they would both have a good laugh about an affair which had been so elegantly executed.

He should never have allowed himself to become so solitary, he should not have withdrawn into the world of words, so that now he had to rely on corrupt witnesses for his sanity. That was the mistake he had made. What reason would his enemies have to tell the truth? None at all. He had despised the ordinary and it had turned round and bitten him. It had turned its aloof mocking face on him, it had played esoteric games with him: he who had thought he was the élitist of the study. Like the far side of the moon with its mysterious hollows and shadows it was blindly turning its cruel face towards him.

The ordinary witnesses whom he had despised were taking their revenge on him, and what a subtle revenge it was, far more subtle than any of his plots. Who would have foreseen it, that ordinary people would be so clever, that after all they recognized that he depended on them for the true colour of an orange, an apple. On them depended his reality. From their dull ponderous hands hung the real world as on a golden chain. An exile, he returned, blinded now and again to that ordinary world from his own world, and it had seemed to be waiting for him harmlessly. But like the corrupt evil fairies they had stolen it away from him. They were more evil than he had ever imagined. He had looked down on them from above as if they were a tribe of busy ants engaged in a bizarre unfathomable business of their own. But all the time they had been glancing at him sideways out of their small ant's eyes and saying to themselves with remorseless bitterness, We will get you yet: Oh we will and no mistake.

Their spiteful little eyes were now all around him like evil stars, mocking and besieging him.

In a short while they would be reaching the house again. He thought of it as a trap, set in a beautiful garden, with the lovely cherry tree in the centre. Linda's eyes were closed and the taxi driver was whistling under his breath 'Bridge Over Troubled Waters'. The road stretched before him, a tape on a tape recorder, the track he must take unless he exerted his will power. They had now passed the hotel and he would soon be at the house and God knew what bizarre scenario was waiting for him there.

The taxi drew up at the house and they all got out of it. But then before Linda or the taxi driver knew what was happening he had run away from them and was walking purposefully towards the town. They couldn't do anything now for there were plenty of cars passing on the road, tourists probably: and in the fields he could see people strolling. He gritted his teeth and ran on. The other two stared after him, panic-stricken, not knowing what to do. They had thought that he would enter the house quite tamely and submit to them but he knew better than that. They would now have a consultation and decide what they could do next. In this complicated chess game he had made an unorthodox move: he had taken himself off the board completely. He headed steadily for the town which was twelve miles away. But though he felt tired that didn't bother him. He wanted to get to his own doctor who would convince him of his sanity. On the right-hand side of the road huge rhododendrons grew freely, in clouds of gaping red. There was also a shimmer of bluebells, hyacinths. This road was very familiar to him. Once he and Linda had seen a fawn, long legged and fastidious and delicate, stepping across it. And one night she had stopped to take care of an owl which had slammed into the windscreen of the car. Oh, she was kind to animals all right. She couldn't bear to leave a dead cat or dead rabbit lying on the road for cars to squash it flat endlessly. No, she had to get out of the car to remove the carcass to the side. There were such paradoxes in her nature: how could one understand human beings at all?

He heard the taxi drawing up behind him but continued walking. The taxi stopped and the driver leaned out of the window.

"Come back home, sir. Don't be a fool."

"Come on," said Linda. "You're making an exhibition of yourself."

"No," Ralph snapped and kept on walking.

"What's wrong?" said the driver. "You have a beautiful wife, a beautiful house. What more do you want?"

"You keep them then," Ralph shouted angrily.

The taxi driver looked angry as if at any moment he would jump out of his taxi and hit him but he wasn't frightened. Not at all. The taxi came to a stop while the two of them consulted with each other as to what they should do next and then it raced onwards and in a short while returned. This time he kept his head down so that he wouldn't see the two of them. He kept on walking, one foot in front of the other, one foot in front of the other. Eleven miles past the bridge, the still waters, in which trees were reflected perfectly, were without motion. If only the world of human beings were like that, serenely painted, but, no, in that world there were all sorts of distortions. There were no true reflections.

A steady stream of cars passed but no one seemed surprised to see him walking. He kept to the grass verge and felt the wind of the cars' headlong humming course. More than ever he was convinced that Linda and the taxi driver were stalking him. Why else should the taxi driver have remained at all? What business was it of his? Why hadn't he gone back to Glasgow? Or was he simply adding mileage so that he could present him with a large bill at the end of his journey? Why indeed had he himself consented to come home at all? He should have stayed where he was, he had allowed himself like a baby to be passive to their will, which was much stronger than his own. Linda had a simplicity and directness of energy which he could never emulate no matter how hard he tried. It was that trait of hers which he admired most but he didn't admire it now, he feared it.

He plodded steadily on. He had settled down into a rhythm now, allowing his feet to take him to his destination, not thinking. That would be best. From the time they had been to Yugoslavia she had thought this plot out carefully: perhaps that was why she had selected Yugoslavia in the first place, had immersed herself in its brochure, nesting with it in her chair. His mind opened frightening vistas. HOW LONG HAD THIS BEEN GOING ON? It hadn't started recently. Mines began to explode in his thoughts, one after the other. When she had come in with cups of coffee for him had she really been deliberately interrupting him, trying to stop the flow of his ideas?

And these endless interrogations about Christianity, had they been intended to unnerve him? Linda, too, was far more superstitious than he was, she believed in planetary influences, ghosts, auras, phantoms. She believed that the Egyptians had encountered space-men in ancient times. She believed that Christ had been a space-man. She believed that planes had disappeared in the Bermuda triangle. She believed that when she died she would go to another planet. Was she not at all frightened of the punishments of hell, then? Did she not feel the flames stroking her hair tenderly? He himself was a rational man, he didn't believe that watches could be bent by minds, he didn't believe that the laws of physics could be set aside by the spiteful winds of magic. He believed that we were all on a perishable road where the grave waited for us, the tombstone with our name inscribed on it like a simple address.

He headed onwards as if into a high wind. And then he heard the car coming up behind him and slowing. It was Linda, but this time Linda on her own without the taxi driver, and in her own car. She drove alongside him as if he were the runner in a race and she was following him with the sustenance of food and water. She leaned out of the window.

"Listen," she said, "I'll take you to the doctor if you must go."

"I don't believe you," he said.

"I swear," she said. "If that is what you want." Cars passed them steadily, in a magnified and diminishing roar, and people looked at the two of them as if wondering what was happening. In one car a tall black dog stood upright as a Buddha, with smooth shining black skin.

"No," Ralph shouted.

"Come on," said Linda. "I won't say anything. I won't even speak to you if you don't want me to."

He thought for a while and then he said, "All right then," and got into the car. He refused to put his safety belt on and Linda didn't say anything. He didn't want to be bound and helpless if she suddenly turned back. But, no, she was indeed driving in the direction of the town. Perhaps she was really telling the truth.

"Where did you meet him," he asked at last.

"Meet who?"

"That so-called taxi driver."

"I've never seen him before in my life."

"That's a laugh. What's he doing helping you then? Why hasn't he gone back to Glasgow?"

"Because he has some human feeling, that's why. He has a wife and six children. He says he's seen this kind of thing before. He's sorry for me, that's why he stayed. And I'm very lucky, that he should have done."

"And where is he now?"

"What do you mean, where is he now? He's probably gone back to Glasgow."

"Probably?"

"I'm sure he's had enough of this. I would if I were him."

"Would what?"

"Have gone back to Glasgow."

"Huh."

He relapsed into his seat beside her. She was like an eel, she had an answer for everything. The terrible thing was that he could prove nothing against her. And she probably had a tape recorder hidden in the car taking down everything he said so that she could use it as proof against him.

"Can't you go faster than this?" he asked.

"If you want," she said, sensing the challenge in his voice. He glanced at her fixed profile as if it were stamped on a false coin.

And then the voice said to him, You must kill yourself and her. Put the car off the road. That is what you must do.

He listened. Why hadn't he thought of it before? That would solve all his problems at once. He didn't care about his own life anyway and as for her, he wanted his revenge. The car was going quite fast now, Linda staring ahead of her, and suddenly in a savage motion he grasped the wheel and began to tug. At first Linda didn't realize what was happening and panicked, not knowing what to do. The car swerved from side to side of the road and then she applied the brakes and he tried to kick her leg away. Another car passed, a man's mouth opening in surprise. Ralph fought like a madman and Linda fought against him for her life. And then the car came to a stop. She ran out of it to another car which had come to a stop as well. He ran after her and then when he saw the other car he slowed down and began to walk away as if he didn't have a care in the world. If those people hadn't been there! But, no, they were looking at him and Linda was standing between them, panting, her face dead white.

He began to run blindly along a path into the wood which lay on the far side of the road. He passed a farmhouse and heard some hens clucking in the yard. A cockerel crew: that was bad luck, for a cockerel to crow in the middle of the day. There were a lot of leaves, roots, trunks of trees dappled with sun. He must get clear of all pursuit. He didn't want to see anyone again. He crossed a park where sheep were grazing and plunged into the wood again. The ground was mossy and soft and his shoes sank into it. Finally he came to a clearing and sat down in it. After a while he lay on his back and stared up at the sky where the clouds passed slowly as if made of marble.

In the middle of the wood. . . . He heard the whisperings of little animals but saw nothing. He sat up, took the bottle of pills from his pocket and began to count them. He poured them into his palm and gazed at them, the little red globes. Before he swallowed them there was something else he felt he ought to do, but he couldn't think what it was. What did people do before they killed themselves? Of course. They left a suicide note. He took out a letter which he had received from South Africa asking if they could use for an anthology a short story of his. Then he scribbled in large letters on the back, the words, MEET YOU IN HELL, and he addressed it to Linda. That would really frighten her. Even if he didn't believe in hell she did and she would wake up in the middle of the night wondering if he was haunting the house. It might take years for them to have that infernal rendezvous but for the rest of her life she would remember his last words.

He arranged some twigs below him. He might as well be comfortable. He might as well look calm and resolute in death. After all, this death might be reported. He might as well die like a classical hero as if he didn't have a care in the world.

He looked down at the pills in his hand. They reminded him of the eggs of a very tiny exotic bird, which sang deep in the middle of the wood. Like the thrush's nest he and Linda had found recently, in the garden, one fairly large green egg in it, but quite cold, for the bird had deserted it. And in any case when they had smelt it, it was rotten. It had been hidden deeply among foliage and twigs. The bird was now somewhere else, regretting its cold green egg, as if it were earth itself.

No one would ever find him here, that was sure. He put all the pills in his mouth and swallowed them quickly lest they should burn his throat, which was dry. Having done that he lay down on his back again and watched the sky. Castles, heads, stones, ruffs, they were all there against a background of transparent blue like the shell of an egg. He smiled bitterly and ironically. So this was what his life had led to, this mess. And yet what a perfection too! Was it not better to take one's own life than submit to the order of nature? He snuggled closer into the green foliage as if it were a blanket or a coverlet. Directly ahead of him he saw a sheep's eye, green as a splintered jewel. It stared directly into his own. A blade of grass hung from the mouth absentmindedly. Shortly his own eyes would close and he would be dead. And he wasn't at all frightened. Not at all. On the contrary he was happy. It was the happiest moment of his life. He had at last taken a decision.

Without his knowing it, his eyes closed. The last thought he had was of Pula, that place in Yugoslavia where the colosseum was. The emperor's thumb was turned down and the heat was blazing intensely inside that stony ring.

Two

BUT THAT OF course was later. First, there was the landing at Pula with Linda and her mother who, at eighty years old, had swollen legs and was suffering from kidney trouble. They landed in the evening, in the dim light, and saw a soldier with a machine gun strapped over his shoulder at the airport. The place seemed strange and frightening, as if they had landed in a ghostly country. In the bus taking them to their hotel Ralph talked to a man from Dundee who worked as a printer on a newspaper. He told him about computers, and how his newspaper office had recently been computerized. It was his first time abroad and he also had his wife and his mother-in-law with him. He had checked out everything in advance and knew exactly when the bus was due to arrive at the hotel. How efficient and bright he sounds, thought Ralph, and I myself feel so heavy and dull and tired. He only half listened to the lady courier in the front of the bus who was describing their route to them. She had an Irish accent.

When they arrived at the hotel they found all the English-speaking residents waiting for them.

"Any newspapers, magazines?" they asked, clustering round them like starving seagulls. "What's happening in the Falklands?"

Ralph handed over all his newspapers and magazines, distributing them like alms to beggars. As yet the final landing had not been made. The fleet was hovering out at sea, while being attacked by Argentinian planes with French Exocets.

They handed in their passports at the desk and took the ancient lift up to their rooms. The receptionist was a German who spoke broken English.

While Linda took her mother along to her room, which was adjacent to their own, Ralph waited, looking out the window at the water which shone with the lights of boats. In the twilight, tourists walked up and down the promenade and in the distance he could hear the sound of music.

He picked up a brochure which Linda had laid on the bed, and leafed through it. It was a good few years out of date and stated that the Yugoslavs had determined to make tourism their main industry. The *per capita* income was low, the economic system not wholly Communist, not wholly Western. As far as he could make out the hotels were run by the state. He wandered about the room and noticed that the plug for the light seemed dangerously exposed. On the back of the door there was a list of the prices in dinars.

When Linda came back he asked her how her mother was.

"Tired. Her legs are badly swollen."

"Will she sleep all right?"

"I've given her her sleeping tablets." While she was answering his questions Linda was taking their clothes from the cases and hanging them in the wardrobe.

"Has she anything to read?"

"She has a *Woman's Realm*. They weren't interested in that. There's nothing about the Falklands in it."

Ralph passed his hand across his brow. He felt desperately tired. At the airport he had been more confused than usual, worrying about his passport and his documents, transferring them from pocket to pocket, checking continually that he still had them. Maybe he had been working too hard: he had never felt as exhausted as this before. He lit another cigarette and noticed that there was a blue ashtray on the dressing-table. Linda was still folding stuff away. Ralph opened the wooden doors and stepped on to the balcony, looking down on the leisurely tourists who were swimming about in the half light. He was assailed as he so often was by the contingency of things, as if Yugoslavia were not a necessary place. Why, he might just as easily be in Greece or in Italy but for some reason Linda had chosen Yugoslavia and he had let her do the choosing, too tired to interfere. He tried to think of any information he might have randomly gathered about Yugoslavia but could think of little. It was not the sort of place that echoed with significances and harmonies.

Linda had now finished packing and was undressing slowly.

"Will you draw the curtains?" she said. And he did so.

"I wonder," said Ralph, "why your mother was so keen on seeing the Alps."

All the way over on the plane her mother had been asking, Have we passed the Alps yet? and when eventually they did so she had gazed down at them as if she had finally made a discovery of the greatest importance.

"There was a teacher she once had," said Linda, "and he used to go on about the Alps."

"Is that right?" said Ralph indifferently. But Linda said nothing more.

He wasn't sure whether his mother-in-law liked him very much. There was a coldness in his nature which she had never taken to. She was used to talk, as was Linda. But what was there to say about the Alps? Nothing. Except that she had reminisced about her schooldays, quoting fragments of poems which she could remember clearly.

"We had this teacher," she had told them. "A lady teacher. And she used to say to us: If you haven't prepared your work go and stand in that corner. We had more people in corners than we had in the class." And she laughed remembering her early days so clearly. But Ralph was not interested. In fact he had heard many of her stories before, but she repeated them as if they were fresh and pristine, as if they had only happened recently.

He switched on the lamp by the bed while Linda switched off the main light. He began to remove his clothes. He felt no sense of renewal or adventure: even though he was in a strange unknown land, his head was dull and heavy.

When they were lying side by side in bed Linda said reflectively, "She was trying to impress you."

"How?"

"By quoting these poems. You know, things like 'The Cuckoo'. She has a good memory."

"She doesn't know what to make of me," said Ralph. And indeed she would sometimes stare at him as if he belonged to another species. He had no little stories, no snippets of news, he was remote and calculating. He was quite sure that she would have preferred Linda to have married someone else, a talkative decisive man, large and generous.

"No," said Linda absently.

And he was suddenly angry with her as if she was implying that the fault lay with him rather than with her mother. Why should he have to listen to these interminable banal stories, that river of reminiscence which flowed so lazily along, without substance. And yet, and yet, wasn't that what was wrong with his own books? They didn't have the warmth and uncalculated diffuseness that they should have. He always had the fear that there was some deep ordinary unpatterned world that he was missing, that he was passing in an arrogance of splendid indifferent light. After all hadn't that critic, whose name he could not now remember, written, "When Mr Simmons discovers the qualities of humanity and warmth he will be a considerable writer." On the other hand, to be warm and human was to run the risk of sentimentality.

"I was talking to a man from Dundee who works on computers," he said. "He has his holiday all worked out. He knows exactly where he and his wife and mother-in-law will be going every day of their holidays." He smiled in a superior manner as if remembering the days of his greenness when he had been an innocent abroad as well. Suddenly he began to create a scenario for his mother-in-law.

"I bet you when she gets home she will say, 'I looked down and there were the Alps. You've never seen anything like them. I could see Hannibal quite clearly and a few of his elephants. What a time they were having of it.' Elephants are not the sort of animals you should take across mountains. They slip on the ice, they're so big." Rivers of monotonous greyness streaming across the Alps, that was what it must have been like. Heavy, dull, persistent.

Linda laughed, and for a moment the two of them were conspirators in a plot he had invented in that strange twilit land. The huge ungovernable Alps, their mother pecking at the Yugoslav food on the plane, not liking it: wondering what the paper bags were for.

"They're for sickness, mother," Linda had told her.

"Your mother was never sick in her life" — stubborn, proud, independent.

And back in her loved garden, surrounded by roses, carnations, azaleas, talking to the other villagers, You've never seen anything like the Alps. Why they reminded me of . . .

"Oh shut up," said Linda in a good-humoured voice and switched off the light by the bed. "You'll be old yourself some day and as a matter of fact I've heard you telling the same stories over and over to your literary friends. You do, you know."

"Perhaps," said Ralph.

"No perhaps about it." And she turned on her side with a quick decisive movement. "Now go to sleep."

Which he did, thinking of the famished residents holding out their claws for his newspapers as if they were stranded on a rock. The fleet trembled in the Atlantic, sitting ducks for Exocets: such bare land to be fought for and taken, such bare meagre land.

The two of them woke up early in the morning, for the sun was shining brightly and it seemed that a day of hope was waiting for them. They sat about in the room for a while and then Linda went to get her mother, who had been up for about two hours sitting on her bed, and now and again watching the pigeons which fluttered about and settled on the balcony.

"I wish I had something to give them," she said to Linda, for at home she had a bird house in the garden in which she put the leftovers from the food, but which at times a rat or cat might climb into.

She told Linda that early in the morning she had seen a large lorry arriving with a crane to lift the big stone flower containers which stood in front of the hotel. "Where do you think they take them?" she asked.

"Maybe to the other hotels," said Linda. "Maybe they change them about. How are your feet?"

"Not so good. They're swollen again."

A copy of *Woman's Realm* lay on the bed, open at the horoscope page.

She took her mother along to her own and Ralph's room and then they all three descended in the lift. The fair-haired German at the reception desk said "Good morning" to them and they went into the dining-room.

They sat down at a table next to the man from Dundee whose name they discovered was Graham. He was dressed in shirt sleeves and shorts, and had a camera on a chair beside him.

"Helen and mother have gone to look for a newspaper," he said, and then added, "Though I don't believe they sell any English newspapers here. Or so I was told by a friend of mine."

"No English newspapers?" said Ralph.

"That's what I was told," said Graham.

Ralph didn't feel like talking to him, in fact he didn't feel like talking to anyone and he was glad when Graham left them, looking boyish and optimistic, his camera slung over his shoulder.

He bit into the adamantine roll which the tall dark-haired waiter had left them. All around him he could hear the voices of Germans.

"Are they French?" asked his mother-in-law.

"No, German."

His mother-in-law ate in silence, chewing desperately, and Linda remarked, "I tried to speak to that waiter. But he didn't answer me: I wonder if they have been told not to be too friendly with the tourists."

"I don't think so," said Ralph. "Maybe they don't have much English. I wonder what that's supposed to be," and he poked moodily at his plate with a spoon.

"You never know," Linda pursued. "Maybe they don't like us because of the Falklands."

"As a matter of fact," said Ralph, "they're supposed to like the English because of the partisans in the last war."

"The partisans?"

"Yes," but he didn't have enough energy to explain to her about them.

He still felt the same bone-tiredness, and was slightly disoriented because of the foreign languages around him. He shouldn't have been working so hard, driven on by a ferocious puritanism. Nor did he much like living in the village which he and Linda had shifted to, to be near her mother. He missed the chance encounters of the town, its unpredictable nature, and felt as if the ferns and bracken were swallowing him up. One day he had lost his glasses while cutting bracken — they had fallen out of his top pocket — and hadn't found them again in the tall devouring greenery. As happened so often with him he saw this loss as symbolic, nature eating the academic and the scholarly. Though he had searched for them feverishly they were forever lost, to be eaten by the rain and the wind.

"Well," he said, "it's time we went out." And all three rose and went outside into the warm morning.

"There's a place next door here," said Linda. "Perhaps we should change some money."

And they went in and waited behind a thickset German in shorts who spoke at great length to the girl behind the counter. What an extraordinarily fine morning it was too! Already the ubiquitous Germans, in their shorts and shirts, were setting off with their expensive cameras, chattering cheerfully and confidently in their alien gutturals.

The sun glittered on the water and on the boats, and far out on the horizon Ralph could see yachts.

They walked slowly along the promenade, stopping at a booth which was run by a woman with a German accent.

"English papers?" said Ralph carefully.

"Nein," she said or some such word. It seemed to Ralph that she spoke contemptuously as if English papers were the last thing she could be expected to keep. He pointed to a packet of Yugoslav cigarettes which seemed extraordinarily cheap according to the calculations he had made, and she handed them over. He opened the packet and lit one. It was awfully cheap-looking, and not packed as tightly as English ones were.

"No wonder they're cheap," he said to Linda.

As they walked along the promenade they came across a German who, fishing in the shallow water, had landed what looked like a small slimy octopus. A little boy came along and examined it with wide eyes as it lay in its purple colour on the stone, dying.

"What's that?" said Linda's mother.

"It looks like an octopus," Ralph said. His mother-in-law was stopping now and again to undo her laces, and then changing her mind and tying them again.

"Aren't you comfortable?" said Linda to her.

"Not really," said her mother. "I've brought the wrong shoes."

"Maybe we should go and buy you some sandals," said Linda.

"If you like. I don't like this place. I should never have come. You young people should have come on your own."

"Not at all," said Linda, glancing at Ralph. "Once we get you proper shoes you'll be all right."

They left the promenade and laid their jackets down under the trees. All along the rocks half-naked people were roasting themselves in the sun. Some of them were big-bellied like beached whales, some slim and elegant. They all lay with their eyes shut, hands folded across their chests, like effigies. The sun was the single overwhelming god they all worshipped.

"Did you notice," said Linda, "that all the big cars are German. The Yugoslavs have small cars. The Germans have big limousines."

"I hadn't noticed," said Ralph.

He had an image in his mind of a world totally devoted to tourism. In that world everyone would be a tourist and no one knew anyone else. There were no indigenous peoples or if there were they were like the Anglo-Saxons under the Normans, hidden in the woods, peering out now and again at the strangers who had taken over their land. Wherever one walked in this world one met only tourists and these tourists were intent on tanning themselves as much as they could and then in the evening sitting out at tables, drinking peacefully and meditatively. Many people could not communicate at all for the languages would all be different and certain places such as famous towers, waterfalls, castles, would become the temples of a new religion. He closed his eyes against the blinding vision and listened to Linda as she said to her mother, "I'll take you along to a shop and find you more comfortable shoes. Ralph, you don't need to come."

Ralph lay in the sun while they were away. Once he watched a party of youths supervised, he thought, by a German, and Germans themselves, horse-playing on the pier, wearing only bathing trunks. As he watched he saw a group of four dragging a protesting youth towards the edge of the pier, then with one huge heave throwing him into the glittering water. He still watched as the youth rose from the water, shaking his head like a dog, and the four who had thrown him in returned to their leader having forgotten already what they had done. They and the leader laughingly pored over a map. After a while the youth came out of the water and padded damply towards the rest of the party, forlorn and loitering, hangdog and ashamed. He joined in with the others and was soon laughing as well, but Ralph as novelist knew that he had not forgotten the incident. In fact he would always remember it: such insults were his destiny. He was the perpetual outsider, wheedling his way back into the group, but never wholly accepted; rather like himself in his own youth.

From such loneliness had he been delivered by Linda into the real world, its terror and its banality. They were together till death did them part, the major death which followed all the minor sharp-toothed deaths. Often her commonsense moved him with its divine accuracy, and her country was a country that he wished that he could inhabit.

He watched as the two of them came towards him along the

70

promenade, Linda holding her mother by the arm. The latter had changed into sandals and was carrying a small parcel which contained, probably, the shoes she had removed.

When they sat down beside him, Linda said, "It was a big shop but their stuff isn't all that good, and quite expensive. Mother doesn't like her sandals either."

"They're not right," said her mother. "I wish I hadn't come here. You young people should be enjoying yourselves."

Here in Yugoslavia she looked old and shrunken, not at all the dominant figure which she was in her own house. She seemed threatened by the nakedness of youth, the sun, the alien languages. There was nothing more threatening than people bent exclusively on pleasure, Ralph thought.

"She thought this German we saw was speaking English," said Linda laughing, "and talked to him about her life as a nurse. But he shook his head at her, waved his hands, and finally she had to give up."

"Well, it did sound like English," said her mother protestingly.

"And anyway," said Linda, "why should he be interested in your nursing career?"

"What's that?" said Ralph suddenly seeing a quick flicker along the wall of the pier, and the disappearance of it among the hot stones.

"Probably a lizard," said Linda. "I've seen a few of them."

Ralph kept his eye on the fissure but the lizard, if lizard it had been, didn't appear again. Confused by the sun and by the variety of things, he wished to be back in his study, remote and cool. The tourist seemed to him to be like the ordinary person, living on what the world supplied from moment to moment, having no central obsession, drifting, seeing now and again a castle or a harbour, which illuminated his day, like a bird which fed on the crumbs scattered for him, not wondering where they came from. How could people live like that? How could people live with no pattern, coming across by chance a new experience, a new incident, accident about which they might talk. His own ghostly figure in his study was more substantial.

Yes, the whole world was a tourist centre, people seeking the final view, the final picturesque castle, the final experience. But as soon as one was seen, tasted, there was another waiting to be investigated, each in its lumpy dumbness, a question-mark

71

waiting to be illuminated. So too was history. The light of brisk consciousness lit Rome, Greece, for a moment then passed on elsewhere.

His mother was removing fragments of stone, sand, from her sandals, and had already loosened them. And Linda was gazing with serene profile towards the water where some youths were swimming.

After a while they ate some food which Linda had bought when looking for the shoe shop. There was an unusual kind of jam which neither Ralph nor his mother-in-law liked. The food tasted different, foreign, unappetizing.

The two of them decided to take their mother back to the hotel and then they themselves would walk among the shops. They left her lying on the bed, the *Woman's Realm* beside her, the pigeons chasing each other on the balcony. They felt guilty leaving her but she insisted that that was what she wanted, she would be all right. Her legs were swelling again. "You young ones must see the place. Don't mind me."

And they went out into the blinding sunlight which was as direct and powerful as a drawn sword, bouncing back from the water and the stone. A primitive place this, old houses with flaking balconies, women sitting on them, perhaps a rose flowering here and there, in a bright flash of red. The walls of the houses were cracked as if the sun had been chewing them for years. Washing hung from some of the balconies. Poor country, how much poorer it was than Britain.

"I wish I had something to read," Ralph said to Linda. "I shouldn't have given away all my papers and magazines last night."

At the back of the town they found what seemed to be the main street, if street it could be called, for it was more like a sunbaked winding path. There were a large number of gift shops, each with its obligatory portrait of Tito, the great man dressed in military uniform, sometimes staring sternly ahead of him, sometimes writing at a desk, his head bowed. In the shops there were many leather goods, and animals made of wood, elephants, horses, dogs. In others there was cheap jewellery. In a chemist's shop they saw an old Yugoslavian woman arguing with a shop assistant who listened smilingly. Ralph would have loved to understand what they were talking about but could only listen and try to interpret the gestures and expressions. He felt uncomfortable and frustrated behind the alien wall of words.

They found a small shop which sold paintings, many of them of the women of the country, others of landscapes brightly and garishly coloured. He was interested to find that the country seemed to be both Catholic and Communist at the same time.

An Italian shouted from an ice-cream shop, in English, "Best ice cream. Best ice cream." He leaned through the window of his shop towards a girl who had stopped to listen. Suddenly he began to throw lumps of ice cream high into the air, catching them again in the scoop with the greatest of ease. His skill was amazingly deft as all the time he was shouting, "Best ice cream, best ice cream." They bought some of the ice cream but didn't like it. It had a greyish appearance and melted rapidly in the intense sunshine, which was now hammering at them with blinding force.

"Don't you think we should go back to the hotel," said Ralph who was sweating profusely. But Linda didn't want to. She could stand the heat much better than he could. They wandered into a museum and strolled from floor to floor. There were ancient Yugoslav artefacts, stone coffins, inscriptions in Latin, some of the words of which had been eroded. There were paintings of Yugoslavs in national costumes. There were seats and chairs covered in velvet, and a room devoted to the Second World War, with maps and charts, an arrow pointing to where the Headquarters had been, and others to where the major battles had been fought.

When they left the museum they went round to the back — Linda in search of a toilet — and found themselves in a garden of roses, fragrant and opulent, while set in the wall were stone heads of Romans, with empty staring eyes.

Linda didn't know any Latin but Ralph knew some and he could decipher some fragments of the inscriptions. It seemed to be a fragmented country, historically broken. There were few Yugoslavs to be seen; he felt like an invader of the country, as if he had no right to be there. And furthermore he missed his reading, for though he had inquired at all the kiosks he could find no books or magazines or newspapers in English.

Linda spent a lot of time trying on a ring but decided in the end against buying it.

In this land Ralph felt more dependent on her than ever before. With terror he imagined her disappearing and himself searching in alien police stations, among alleys, in formal offices, and not being able to find her. He was disappointed in the town, all these slums, cracked and broken, the vases with roses on the balconies. So meagre everything was, so dull and poverty stricken. They couldn't find a restaurant with proper English food anywhere. He wandered about as in a dream, a tired hot automaton.

He began to invent stories. In one there were two schoolmistresses who had come to Yugoslavia and who hated each other. One was weak, one was strong. The strong one disappeared and the weak one eventually found her hiding among the roses and the heads of Roman emperors. She slapped her face in anguish and dislike. In another a little boy swam out towards a ghostly yacht in the bay, freeing himself from his estranged quarrelling parents. It seemed to him that he must create fables, tales, fantasies, to make the world real, otherwise there would only be the gift shops, the baked clayey roads, the shops in which patient Yugoslavs sat, immured in their foreign language, watching the rich strutting tourists.

Eventually they returned to the hotel as the heat had become fierce and oppressive. They lay down on their bed side by side and after a while fell asleep.

For a day or two this pattern continued, though sometimes the two of them would sit in their mother's room in the afternoon, sheltering from the heat. While the other two talked, Ralph would find himself reading the *Woman's Realm*, as there was no other reading matter available. He read a story about a blind woman who had been involved in a plot against her life in Greece, a plot labyrinthine and almost impenetrable: and another one set in a hospital. He read the letters' page in which girls confided that they had fallen in love with married men, and asked what they should do about it. Others complained of boy friends and husbands having affairs. What was to happen about houses after separation? Some houses were in the husband's name, some in the wife's. There were so many people to whom so many horrible things happened. Some were given no housekeeping money, some wondered about their children who were on drugs or sniffing glue, some wrote in to say that their husbands were now retired and following them about the kitchen. It was a catalogue of minor tragedies. Young girls wrote in to say that they were too shy to talk to anyone; how could they improve their conversational techniques? Others worried about the spots on their faces, the shape of their noses, the size of their breasts. They cried out for the definitive remedy for fatness, thinness, ugliness, they looked for the ultimate oracle. Ralph turned over the pages casually: everywhere there was a cry for help.

He disliked more than anything his lack of reading material. He had never been so long without books. He wanted to know what was happening in the Falklands, he wanted to know about Yugoslavia itself. Who were the people who governed it? What did they think of Britain? What sort of education system did they have? Did they have a Health Service? What did the people do with themselves, for he never saw any of them in the vicinity of the hotel which was totally devoted to tourists. Could he hear any of their stories, listen to any of their native songs or ballads? He was reduced to the meagre minimal sights of the day, watching the Germans draw out from the kerb in their large gleaming limousines.

Once, on a day which was heavy and cloudy with lightning and thunder and rain, he saw three men dressed in long white gowns dancing about in the teeming puddles, one with a rose in his hand. Were they tourists? Yugoslavs? There was no way of knowing. They seemed to be drunk and hugely enjoying themselves. Then they got into an old car and drove away, regally waving.

And as they sat in their mother's room she would tell them stories of her past while resting her legs, which were wreathed with varicose veins, and swollen.

"When I was a nurse in Edinburgh we had this strict matron. She wouldn't allow us to meet our boy friends. But we went out just the same through the windows. One night when we were coming back to the hospital we heard her talking to this man in the garden. She had a boy friend of her own and never told us. She was dressed in her best, too.

"There was a boy who was dying of TB and he wrote a poem for me. I still have it. One minute he was joking with me and the next he was dying in my arms."

And then, "Did you see that waiter? Linda talked to him one night but he was taken away. He never comes to our table now. They don't want us to talk to them, that's what it is."

Ralph sat and listened. He felt himself dying of an intolerable boredom. Sometimes they all three would spend a long time studying the pigeons and throwing out fragments of hard roll on to the balcony. There was one particular pigeon, fierce and masterful, which managed to get all the food for itself, driving all the others away. He would flutter his wings in a menacing manner and the other birds would retreat from him. Ralph called him Tito.

And all the time their mother would say, "You young ones should be enjoying yourselves. You shouldn't be staying in with me."

But in fact there was nothing to do. There was no cinema, no theatre. Only excursions to other parts of Yugoslavia, and to Italy. The Grahams went on one of these every day and in the evening would tell them where they had been. They looked fresh and endlessly inquisitive, and the old mother was alert and spry. In the morning they would set off with cameras and bags: in the evening they would stroll in the crowded streets.

Ralph found that he could no longer invent stories, that he was nailed to the tedium of the day like a cross. Now and again he would see an old native woman dressed completely in black walking along the pavement. What had she not seen, what wars, what horrors, what atrocities? And yet she paced so stolidly by the water, "Just like the women at home used to be," said his mother-in-law.

She herself looked young and slim, dressed in slacks. What Ralph would have given to talk to these old women, but there was no way in which he could do so. Sometimes the old woman in black had a child by the hand.

At times his mother would say, "I hope the garden will be all right. I hope Mary won't forget to water the plants."

One day, while they were having their lunch at a table in the open air, they met a couple from England. The man had just recovered from a major operation and was returning to another one when his holiday was over. He was a clerk and on Sundays umpired amateur cricket matches. Linda's mother told them of her nursing days and they listened politely. While they were talking, Ralph had an image of the clerk umpiring a cricket match in Yugoslavia, while the sun beat blindingly down. On one side were Englishmen dressed in cool flannels, on the other were Yugoslavs dressed in brigandish cloaks or military uniforms, and carrying bandoliers of ammunition, grenades. Neither side could communicate with the other and the game degenerated into a brawl. The clerk talked on and on, watched solicitously by his wife. "My boss said, You take as much time off as you want. You have been with us for years, for years." And the wife said, "It was a major operation. Five hours. And they didn't know what was wrong with him. They still don't. When he goes back he has to have another operation."

Later, Linda's mother said, "Cancer. Without a doubt. I've seen it before. They go a papery colour."

Ralph felt sorry for the clerk though he had hardly spoken to him. It was with great difficulty that he could find anything to say, and hardly spoke to Linda and her mother. He blamed this on his isolated days as a writer when he met no one except the creatures of his imagination. But Linda thought that he was aloof and inhuman and selfish. "You're just not interested in people. I don't understand you at all."

As a matter of fact Ralph felt that he was in a foreign country as far as Linda's mother was concerned. It was as if he couldn't speak her language nor she his. She would read the letters in *Woman's Realm* and believe implicitly in the answers given. Or she might read an article on fitness in which the writer compared the human body to a car and say, "That is true enough. I never thought of that before. You have to look after yourself as you look after a car." In her youth she had driven a car but was too old to do so now.

"Do you see that man over there?" she would say. "He's from Scotland," though to Ralph it was quite clear that he was a German.

He couldn't imagine how Yugoslavia appeared to her. She seemed to think of it as a maze which she tried to ignore by talking about the days of her youth. She would only become animated when she was perhaps sitting in a park among flowers.

"We haven't flowers like that at home," she would say. "No. But then they don't have our flowers either."

To her these statements of the utmost banality sounded like epigrams. And Ralph would talk to Linda about her.

"Why is it that she tells the same stories over and over again," he would say.

"Well, she's old. You must understand that."

"No, it's not that. She was doing that before she became old. She never tires of the same stories. She thinks that the Yugoslavs consider us to be spies and that is why they took our passports the first morning."

"Maybe they do."

"Of course they don't."

The odd thing was that there were hardly any policemen to be seen. Surely there ought to be more of them in a Communist state.

"Perhaps they don't need them," said Linda. "Perhaps they spy on each other, report on each other. Have you noticed though that people here don't bother locking their cars. Nobody seems to steal anything. I bet we could leave our room open and find everything untouched."

Instead of growing more relaxed as a result of sleeping most afternoons, Ralph found himself growing more and more tense. These afternoons seemed to take whole years to pass, and when he woke from his sleep he felt unrefreshed and bad-tempered. The air felt heavy and muggy and there didn't seem to be a breeze of wind at any time.

He studied the Yugoslav waiters and waitresses. When they were serving the customers they spoke little but among themselves they laughed and giggled like children. A thickset woman like Krushchev, belly thrust forward like the prow of a ship, strode into the hotel every morning and talked to the waiters and waitresses. Was it her job to superintend the hotel? Was she some kind of commissar? The waitresses themselves in their white blouses and black skirts were sexless, aloof, as if they were fulfilling a duty and not enjoying it.

"Did you hear," said Linda, "that the night we came one of our group fell on the stairs and broke his leg. He was taken to hospital."

"No, I didn't hear that."

"He's all right now. They put his leg in plaster. You sometimes see him hobbling about the hotel."

"How did they treat him?"

"Quite well, I think."

"I shouldn't like that," said Ralph. "It would be awful. To be in hospital in a foreign country."

"Perhaps I shouldn't have taken mother," said Linda. "She's not well. Her legs swell every night. She doesn't feel happy here."

"To tell you the truth," said Ralph, "I don't feel very happy myself. If only there was something to read. The days are so long. And there's an odd sort of barrier here, I can sense it. It's not simply the language. They don't want to have anything to do with us."

Tito, competent and aloof, sitting at his desk writing, reminded Ralph of his own cool and aloof and remote stepfather, who would retire behind a book or newspaper shutting Ralph out by a frozen silence, especially if he had committed some misdemeanour.

"Tomorrow we're going on a cruise. Remember?" said Linda.

"I haven't forgotten. Have you got the tickets?"

"In my bag."

"Perhaps you should check that they're there."

"That's the fourth time you've asked me to do that. I don't need to."

Ralph was angry with himself. He was always saying to her, Make sure that the passports are in the case, that our travellers' cheques haven't been stolen. He had never felt so nervous before. What was wrong with him? Had he been overworking? True, there had been that article that he had had to write very quickly before he could set out on his holiday. And then there were these sudden nervous sweats when he poured with perspiration for no apparent reason. And then of course he had come to a stop with his novel.

"I'm coming to depend on you more and more, and I despise myself for it," he said to Linda.

"Nonsense, you're not dependent on me at all."

"Ever since we married. It's as if I'd given my life into your own hands for safe keeping while I got on with my writing."

"Rubbish."

"But it's true. I was always like that. If there was someone near at hand who would take responsibility I would let them have it. And you have enough to do with your mother."

"It doesn't bother me. But you should speak more to people. To the Grahams, for example."

"But I don't know what to say to them."

"If you were interested in them you would find something to say. The fact is, you're not interested. I think Graham is frightened of you."

"Of me? Why?"

"Well, he thinks of you as being very cosmopolitan. That's why he has to over-compensate by being very efficient. He is terrified of making a mistake and he can't relax. He thinks you are secretly laughing at him."

"I'm not laughing at him."

"You have to remember that he is very young."

"I'm not laughing at anybody."

"Speak to him then. Talk to him."

But though Ralph quite liked Graham he didn't want to speak to him or to anyone else he met. Which was why Linda would say to him, "I can't understand a novelist who doesn't like people. There's something wrong with that."

And for that matter Ralph agreed with her. There must be something wrong with him if he didn't like people. But still Graham was so naive. He went out every morning with his womenfolk as if he was on safari with his shorts and his camera. He looked so fresh and almost adolescent. And he had everything so organized. And it seemed he was really enjoying Yugoslavia. Sometimes he and his wife would tell Linda and Ralph, "Mother gets her tea in bed every morning when we're at home." And the old lady would smile and follow her son-in-law wherever he went. She was self-possessed and as far as Ralph could see had no illnesses or diseases.

And Graham would say, "We're thinking of taking one of the local buses today. I've got a local timetable here." Or, "I found out that the courier is from Sligo. She married a Yugoslavian but she's divorced now."

He knew everything and Ralph knew nothing, and Linda would sometimes say to him, "Why didn't you find out about the local buses?"

"I'm not interested."

"And why do you think yourself too good for the Grahams? He works a computer, you know."

"I know. I don't feel myself too good for him. It's just that he's so damned apple-cheeked and optimistic."

But in fact all he wanted to do was to avoid Graham and find a book and read it. In spite of that he had to listen to the conversation of the people at the tables. But though he waited in the foyer for more tourists to come off the bus at night they wouldn't give him their magazines or newspapers: they kept them for themselves as if they had known in advance of the sparsity of reading material. They were mean and avaricious. He was reduced to reading the notices on the notice boards which told of the excursions that were planned.

One evening in the coolness when all three of them were strolling along the promenade Ralph had the most frightening sensation. He felt as if the landscape around him was falling apart, that it was spinning on its axis. He put his hand on his head and stood still for a long time, while the sea beyond him surged and swayed, the yachts turned keels over sails in the water. A man wearing a tartan cap was landing from one of the pleasure boats, and dancing on the pier while the rest of the passengers cheered and shouted. But Ralph sensed that the world was racing away from him at tremendous speed, that he was being left behind, that the people who were lying roasting themselves on the rocks were ghosts from another country, that he himself was entirely alone and lost, that pages of books were swirling on a cold breeze which had suddenly sprung up, that he couldn't keep his balance.

"Are you all right?" said Linda.

"Yes, yes, I'm fine." He didn't want to tell her that he wasn't all right, he wanted to be always self-sufficient and remote. Too much talk leaked his virtue away.

But above all he saw again the old cruel heads of the Romans staring from among the roses as if passing judgement. They would never have bothered about his mother-in-law with her swollen legs and varicose veins. They would never have listened to her banal stories, her death would not have troubled them. They would have been concerned with power, with the spear, with the javelin, with the march of the legions.

The day they went on the fish picnic was one of their better, more enjoyable, days, as it was also their first excursion. The boat called at various small piers on the way, to pick up men and women from the hotels which lay along the waterfront. There were a large number of Germans, Swedes, and a group of Scots wearing tartan tammies, though none wore a kilt. After a while the Scots, led by a tall egotistic man who, Linda later discovered, was from Glasgow, began to sing Scottish songs while a humble Yugoslav musician with an accordion, weaving in and out among the passengers, tried to play the tunes, Loch Lomond among them. The voyage itself was relaxing and once they passed some nudists who were strolling among the rocks: one man in particular caused huge gusts of hilarity and a concerted rush to cameras because he was sitting like a gnome fishing off a cliff wearing nothing but a pair of bright yellow wellingtons.

"I've seen bare bums before," said Linda's mother, "I don't know what all the fuss is about."

On board the boat was a Frenchwoman who wore a beret and a short skirt, and who at first sat beside a vacantly smiling peaceful man who, Ralph presumed, was her husband. Suddenly she got to her feet and began to dance furiously by herself on the deck, waving her arms, flicking her fingers, hitching up her skirt, making funny faces and thrusting out her false teeth. Her energy was quite ferocious as, watched by her long-suffering husband and encouraged by the Scots, she pushed out her bottom in an improvised version of the can-can till she was joined by the leader of the Scots contingent who was determined that she should not outdo the natives of a country which was, after all, famous for its music and song. Always there is one of them, an exhibitionist, thought Ralph, who instantly created the story of the French husband and wife, the former sitting on a bench, a bag on his lap which his wife had left with him and looking around him with a fixed smile on his face as if trying to give the impression that he was proud of his wife, and that she did not at all embarrass him.

Linda was sitting restlessly beside him and then before Ralph could say anything to her she too had sprung to her feet and was dancing a duet with the Frenchwoman, thrusting out her false teeth like a vampire, hitching up her skirt, and staring down at her feet while dancing the reel on the deck of the Yugoslav ship, the Germans and Swedes watching intently but making no attempt to join in themselves.

Ralph was furious and turned away from the obsequious Yugoslav accordionist who was bending towards him, a large happy smile on his face, while he tried desperately to follow the tunes which the Scots were now singing in concert. God damn you, thought Ralph, why must you thrust yourself into the centre of things, why must you be so dramatic, so theatrical? And he began to grow jealous of the Scot from Glasgow who, large and tall, was conducting the Scots in renderings of 'Amazing Grace' and 'O Flower of Scotland'. Linda had by this time completely forgotten about himself and her mother who sat side by side on the bench, the mother gazing tolerantly at her daughter, Ralph inwardly seething.

The Frenchwoman and Linda were vying with each other as to which of the two would invent the most outrageous games. The Frenchwoman took a comb from her hair and began to play on it. Immediately Linda played a biro like a flute. The French-woman draped a scarf around her face through which her large false teeth protruded. Linda removed her shoes and played them like castanets banging them against each other and dancing in her stocking soles. Ralph was angered by their spontaneous creativity, the marvellous inventiveness of the props which they had discovered in the most ordinary of objects.

And all the time he watched the Frenchwoman's husband, who also wore a beret, and who sat patiently with the bag in his lap, as if he were the wife and she the husband. Did he spend his days like this on cruises watching his wife entertaining the passengers, becoming an instant star in the transient world of tourism. Ralph sympathized with the Frenchman and wished that he were able to talk to him. There was a glitter from the two women like the glitter of water along the reaches between islands.

> 'O flower of Scotland' (sang the Scots)
> 'when shall we see your likes again
> who fought and died for
> your own bit hill and glen.'

The Frenchwoman exchanged her beret for a tartan tammy, and marched up and down the deck playing imaginary bagpipes. To be like that, for grace to descend on one, for the deck suddenly to become the theatre of the moment, the bare wooden boards, for it to flower with meaning! Suddenly the Frenchwoman sighed and entirely exhausted sat down to be followed later by Linda. She looked sideways at Ralph as she sat down but he was determined not to speak, prim, pompous, silent.

"I wasn't going to let that Frenchwoman get away with anything," she said at last as if in self-justification.

"Why did it have to be you?" said Ralph angrily.

"You're always so," she searched for a word, " — academic."

"I know how to conduct myself."

"You can't bear to see people enjoying themselves."

"Why does it always have to be you?"

Linda who was now furious maintained a prickly silence. So they sat side by side in their chairs while the boat cut its way through the water, both equally bad-tempered. If only I had something to read, thought Ralph, but there was nothing to do but stare at the green land stretching down to the shore, and at the empty sea. The tourists with their blank demanding eyes bothered him. There was such a lack of pattern to everything around him. He could not assimilate this unknown unstoried land.

Linda and her mother talked about the clothes the women wore, and ignored him. He felt panicky as if he was incapable of creating a plot which would incorporate these people, this land. It intruded itself on him in a raw undifferentiated unstylish lumpish mass. The only image he had found was that of the angling tourist in his bright yellow wellingtons. He had been like a strange foreign bird with a yellow beak, pecking in alien waters.

After a while the boat landed at a pier and the whole party left it and entered the grounds of a restaurant. There, fish was being fried in the open air, while the tourists sat round on wooden benches. Ralph and Linda ate their platefuls of fried fish, which was delicious, in a hostile silence.

"Listen," said Linda fiercely. "You're an élitist, that's what's wrong with you. You never act spontaneously. You're always afraid of making a fool of yourself." That was how she felt about him. His face and head were like those of the Romans who had glared out of the stone among the roses, cruel, remorseless, eyes in stony sockets immune to pain. He glanced at his mother-in-law's labyrinth of varicose veins, rivers which gathered in blue knots, failed aqueducts. And even as he did so she said that she wished to go to the toilet and Linda took her by the arm. The body, how weak, how contingent it was; we carried it about with us with its smell of mortality. Only the soul was unchanging, triumphant. He put the bones beside him on the plate. He looked out towards the sea in search of seagulls but there were none to be seen. He had hardly seen any since coming to Yugoslavia.

In the quiet of the evening, as the ship made its way back, he was still angry. He and his mother and Linda drank Yugoslav brandy and slowly became tiddly. The Scots sang 'Auld Lang Syne', people formed a ring on the deck, the humble accordionist played as best he could, his soft sweaty face smiling continually. Paper hats were given out and Linda wore hers at a swaggering angle. In a strange way Ralph felt as if he was going home, as the sun slanted across the water which was pure and simple and beyond the boundaries and margins and legends of particular nations.

Ralph suddenly conceded that he had been jealous.

"Who of?" said Linda amazedly. "Surely not of that man from Glasgow."

So they made up, in the tranquillity of the moving seascape. It was one of those moments which in the nature of things can't last, harmonious, satiated. Clouds burned in the west. For that moment Scandinavians, Germans, Scots, were together in the mournful inaccurately played music, and as they climbed on to the pier when they had reached their destination it was as if each was leaving a friend behind. In their rakish pirate caps they emerged on to the grey quay.

They walked into the hotel and to a late dinner. The Grahams were still at their table. Ralph found that he could speak to them quite easily through his haze of brandy. He was not aware that he and Linda were laughing very loudly as they told the story of their day.

"So it's mishmash again," they said, looking down at their plates, and they laughed loudly. Graham told them of a man who, while they had been away, had been found trying to smash his morning roll with a hammer; he had been sitting like a workman on the stair.

This image produced more immoderate laughter. Everything suddenly became dramatic, enjoyable, larger than life. Even the waiter smiled at them and spoke in broken English. "Scotland," he said and smiled radiantly. If only, thought Ralph suddenly, we could speak to each other, each of us, beyond language, seeing through souls and bodies as if they were bones of fish.

The Grahams told of another man who had broken his false teeth on one of the morning rolls, and who had gone off in search of a dentist, past workmen driving the yellow dinosaur beaks of excavators. Everywhere apparently there was building and rebuilding. Yugoslavia was creating a world for tourists to live in and hiding behind it. Where were its songs, its own myths? The man who had broken his false teeth waited for hours outside an office and had finally left in disgust.

Suddenly a German woman, stern and thin, leaned over towards their table and said, "Too loud, too loud. Louden laughter." Linda said, "Guten morgen, Sourpussen," and smiled at her brilliantly, as if she were paying her a compliment. The Grahams smiled. Graham took out his wallet and recited his itinerary for the following day.

Suddenly Ralph felt deflated again. The bloody German woman. It occurred to him for the first time that he had taken too much to drink, that in the glow of the brandy he was behaving like a hoodlum, that he was the image of the Scotsman who had sung and danced on the boat.

He heard an English voice saying, "They haven't made the landing yet. They're sitting ducks. What are they waiting for?"

The Hermes was out in the water, distant, aloof, an apparently impregnable castle towards which enemy missiles were heading, vulnerable just the same. In that harsh sweating weather the ships heaved far from home. Even the water underneath was unsafe. The missiles like fish searched and homed, sped through the sea. No, not even the Hermes was safe.

"We're going to Venice tomorrow," said Graham.

"Oh. I'm sure you'll like that."

"We leave at eight in the morning." His wife and mother smiled. They had it all prepared.

Ralph heard one Scotswoman saying to another one, "That's whit they should dae. Have hydrofoils on the Clyde. Fancy that, eh?" And she bared her teeth and laughed. "Only the weather's no sae guid."

The tall waiter in his white jacket stopped at their table. "Glasgow," he said, and put his fingers to his lips, "Mm." He blew a kiss as if in a melodramatic opera.

"That was the best day yet," said Linda, sighing and removing her pirate hat as they took the lift to their floor.

Later, Linda washed some of their clothes and hung them out on the balcony to dry. They padded in bare feet about their room. Down below they could see people sitting at tables drinking slowly and calmly in the gathering darkness.

"Forgive me?" said Linda.

"Of course."

Ralph did not feel at all disoriented in the glow of the brandy. Objects seemed to be in their correct places. Nevertheless he took a sleeping pill as usual, washing it down with water lest it burn his throat.

One of the things that bothered Ralph was that his bone tiredness, which he had now felt for a long time, months, perhaps years, was not melting away in the hot sun. On the contrary it seemed to grow heavier and heavier and though he slept on the bed in the afternoons and had another long sleep at night it remained. There were flashes too of something worse than tiredness, a feeling of the essential meagreness of reality, of its superficial nature, as if it were composed of sun beating on rock, and the human soul itself were a tourist. Books no longer protected him from the barrenness of a world without myth, without story, which belonged to a language that he didn't understand.

One day the three of them were sitting in a park around noon watching another hotel being built. It rose quickly into the sky — even a day seemed to make a noticeable difference — the workmen ran about the skeleton framework, never stopping for refreshment as British workmen did. It seemed absurd to him that they should be building for foreigners, creating luxuries which they themselves would not be able to enjoy. In the middle of their own national world was this other secret world. (Ralph's mother-in-law had the fixed idea in her head that the reason their passports had been examined and taken from them that first morning was that they were being spied on: and that the woman shaped like Krushchev was also a spy.)

As they sat in the park they saw one of the waitresses from their hotel taking her child to a woman who presumably was its grandmother and after kissing and hugging it leaving it with her. So busy these waitresses were, so hard they worked! The granny sat down on a bench and took out a piece of knitting while the

87

child, a girl, sat down beside her. In front of them was a swing on which another girl was composing huge arcs, pushing herself up towards the sky which was a perfect blue. Ralph watched her with a vague interest.

She seemed a determined little girl, perhaps eleven years old or so. At first she didn't want to let the other girl on to the swing at all till the granny went over and spoke to her. But then she did, and returned to her swinging. Her face was resolute and pale as she tried desperately to beat her own previous arc, to rise ever higher and higher, as if she wanted to fly into the very heavens which were so unfadingly blue. From a street across the way an old woman watched from a window in which a vase with roses was set, and in front of her the workmen scurried like birds among the iron branches of the half finished hotel. All around was activity, purposeful, thrusting, and yet, Ralph thought, essentially absurd. These birds were building nests for others on whose foreign alms they existed.

And he could not communicate with any of them. Not the workmen, not the granny or the child on the swing or the other one shyer and more amenable to bullying. So little he really knew about this land, its inner logic, its inner purposes. In splendid arc after arc the girl swung towards the empty sky.

He watched as a little boy came along and asked to use the swing but the girl didn't seem to like him and soon they were throwing stones and twigs at each other while the other girl returned to her granny who was still patiently knitting. In a fury of words which Ralph couldn't understand the boy and the determined girl chased each other round and round the swing which was now moving gently with its initial impetus. The girl pursued the boy and then went back to the swing where she rode the sky in solitary glory. Soon more and more children appeared and she joined them, the resolute leader. The children gathered in a ring around the pale boy and shouted what Ralph took to be a version of 'Cowardy Cowardy Custard' and the boy ran away past the bench on which the three of them were sitting wiping tears from his eyes. This day he would remember forever, the day of his defeat, unless he re-ordered it and made it into a fantasy in which he himself had been the victor. Ralph fantasized that some day he might become a cutting critic of, for instance, drama, of the community that he had been driven from. His wit would protect him instead of his fists, he would become the terror of the stage.

Linda was more concerned with the child's immediate welfare than Ralph was. She beckoned him over to give him a dinar or two but he shook his head and walked on steadfastly. The granny, who seemed to act as a one-woman nursery school, still sat knitting: she had seen worse disasters than this. The Yugoslavs, Ralph noticed, were very fond of their children, always kissing them and petting them: and the children on the whole were well dressed and neat.

Sometimes he would say to Linda, "I don't like this country."

"Why not?"

"I don't know. I feel a hostility. I can't explain it."

"Hostility?"

"Yes. As if they resented us. As if they resented what they have to do in order to earn their living."

"I think you're imagining things. It's just that you don't know the language."

"No, it's more than the language. It's as if they lived in a secret world and I can't reach them."

It was like living in a land before the invention of books, arts. Its blunt barren surface repelled him, the remorseless glitter of its sun. It was as if here for the first time he had been brought face to face with an immutable almost unendurable reality, unprotected from its harsh glare. Above them was that perfect egg-shell azure, like armour. It bothered him far more than it did Linda, while his mother-in-law was more concerned with her ailing flesh. Even the beautiful women, stretched out on rocks, baking to a consistency of brown, did not trouble his flesh. They didn't seem human at all: here the flesh was everything. He felt that his soul was departing from him, dying, white as an egg, in this tropical heat. The sun itself was an emperor of the day, a star actor in this unplotted drama. It seemed to have cracked most of the houses, driven people to shelter in the afternoons, heated the stones, till they were like cinders.

"Actually," said Linda, "I was talking to that courier and she said that though the houses don't look at all attractive they are all beautifully furnished, and all have washing machines."

"It's not that," said Ralph. "What I am trying to get at is the quietness and the greyness. I would hate to live in a country like this. There's some risk, adventure, missing." And indeed in the

89

end he preferred the violence, chanciness, extreme luxury and extreme poverty of the west — even if it included pornographic magazines, strip clubs, madness — to this prevailing drabness. It was like living in a perpetual Sunday. It was almost as if niceness itself could be dispiriting.

"I *want* to be vulnerable," he suddenly said to Linda. And the words came to him as a revelation. He wanted to swing towards the sky at the expense even of grief, sorrow and even death. He wanted to create fictions at the raw edges of things. And at that very moment he said to Linda as he was continually saying, "What have you done with our passports? Have you got them?"

"You know I left them in the case. You're always asking that."

"I don't know why I keep doing that. I didn't use to."

Linda didn't reply. As he gazed at her profile he asked himself, "How well do I know you? Do I know you any better than I know this country Yugoslavia? Is your language as opaque to me as this language here?"

There were times when he didn't understand her womanly moods, the way that her eyes would suddenly brim with tears, and her lips tremble.

She would say to him, "Do you love me? Do you love me? Do you really love me?" Of course he loved her: why should she need to be reassured? Sometimes in the middle of the night she would waken up and say, "I dreamt that vampires were drinking my blood." Her dreams were substitutes for his own novels.

"I was on this island," she told him once, telling him one of her dreams. "And there was a record playing 'Irene Good Night', and I was with relatives. We were all sitting by a stream in the middle of the night and I realized that they were witches. They gave me a drink and I knew that it was drugged and that they were witches. Later I was standing in a garden and I threw the drink among the roses. They were looking at me oddly but I knew that they were my enemies." The story went on and on and he listened to it with horror. Was he really drinking her blood? Was he concerned only with his own narratives, their purity, their authenticity? The characters in his books he could manage but her he could not understand. And often too he would listen to her mother who would say, "Stand up for your rights," and in the next breath "You can't afford to quarrel with your bosses. There's nothing now but officers. In my day there were only sisters and matrons."

The contradictory nature of language and experience! How could he control it, how could he contrive one seamless garment of inner logic? But life wasn't like that, it flooded all banks, it had no reason, no logic, it was simply itself, a gift, that was all that could be said about it.

(Actually two days later they were sitting in a restaurant in Porec and suddenly they heard, tinnily played in a foreign intonation, the record 'Irene Good Night', and Linda turned and looked at him, her face suddenly pale and overwrought: and he himself was startled as if the laws of reality had been broken.)

"I think," said Linda suddenly, "we should go to Venice tomorrow."

"Venice?"

"Yes. Why not?"

"But your mother. Does she want to go to Venice?"

"Why shouldn't she? She wants to go. Don't you, mother?"

"How do we go?" said her mother.

"By boat, of course. We leave early in the morning. I was looking at a brochure."

Venice. Why, of course they would go to Venice. They couldn't surely go home without having visited Venice.

"And then there are the caves," said Linda. "Another day we could go to the caves. There's plenty we could do." If her mother's shoes were all right, if they fitted.

Linda's energy astonished Ralph. Her daring. So much he had read about Venice, so many paintings he had seen. The canals, the gondolas, the domes. Why of course Venice transcended the meagreness of reality, it represented the colourful brilliance of art, music. Such questions as his mother's shoes, her varicose veins, would be overcome there, in the glory of the soul, rising towards the eternal blue of the sky.

"Yes," he said, "of course we'll go to Venice."

And suddenly they had a future again. Their feet pointed in a fresh direction. They would feed like children at that great city which awaited them.

In the morning they were at the pier early, and had to show their passports. Their guide told them that they were only allowed a certain amount of money, but that the ladies could shove some down their bras. When the great white ship left they all three sat on a seat on the deck. Their journey was quiet and uneventful and finally they were drawing alongside a pier. When they left the ship the heat hit them like a drawn sword and they kept together lest they should lose their guide, a young girl who held a red parasol aloft so that they could follow her more easily. They climbed steps and crossed bridges. The sunlight was a searing glitter. Ralph noticed that his mother-in-law was holding her handbag close against her side for she had heard of Italian thieves. Now and again they would glimpse canals to the right and left of them, and people reclining in gondolas. The water looked a dirty green.

Venice. The word was like a spell but Ralph couldn't fit what he saw into the previous picture he had had of it. The houses were less impressive than he had expected, and somehow lacking in solidity, unlike the huge buildings of, for example, London. The city appeared unreal. Now and again he would see the red flash of a flower on a broken balcony. His mother-in-law's face was a confusion of reds and whites.

After what seemed a long time, especially in the pitiless heat, they arrived in St Mark's Square which was a blizzard of pigeons. Above him Ralph could see the famous clock tower with the metallic hammer about to strike. He noticed mangy effigies of lions. Everything seemed cheap and touristy as if the city were the backdrop of a decaying theatre.

The guide pointed to a shop and told them that they could change their money there. Linda went in followed by Ralph and came out with twenty thousand lira. The guide said that the first stop on their itinerary was a glass factory but Linda said to Ralph, "Do you think we should follow her or make our way round Venice on our own?"

"Whatever you like," said Ralph.

"I wish you would make up your mind for once," she hissed at him, but he didn't answer. The guide said that St Mark was supposed to be buried in the church in the square.

"I never read that in the Bible," said his mother-in-law, sitting down on some steps at the side of the church. A large woman sat near them eating a clay-coloured cone which melted in the heat. Pigeons' droppings were broken stars on the stone.

Their mother thought that the woman was Scottish but Linda knew that she was German. Ralph leafed through a guide book which he had bought on the boat. Mistakes were on every page:

"Being built on the water, Venice owes to the lagoon not only its historic events but the very rhythm which rules its tides daily."

"As if a ship anchored in a quiet harbour it gave ospitality to clever men, famous artists and sensitive souls."

"If you come by plain you will reach the airport Marco Polo at Tessera."

"The traffic in the canals is very typical: it takes place mainly by gondola, a boat of very old origins."

"We hope this wonderful city may appear to the visitor like a fantastic vision, and clear and hearty . . ."

The very language seemed to reflect in its carelessness the untidiness that Ralph saw everywhere, the glitter, the cheap gold-coloured glitter.

Finally Linda suggested they should have a look at the shops and they walked from one to another trying to remember their position in relation to the square. She, like Ralph, had expected some remote beauty, marbly and unapproachable, but not this glare, this tawdry rubbish, the gaudy paintings all outrageously expensive, the trashy silvery models of gondolas. Nor did she particularly like the Italians. When she picked up an English newspaper from a stand and having glanced at it replaced it again the newsagent had stared at her in a hostile manner as if she should have bought it.

After a while they arrived at a restaurant in front of which were some seats. She chose a table under a large red canopy but when the waiter came over and said that an ice cream would cost the equivalent of a pound she rose to her feet and stalked indignantly away.

Her mother however chose this moment to want to go to the toilet and as there were no public toilets Linda had to ask the restaurant owners if she could use theirs. They were distinctly unfriendly and it was only when Linda gave them a few of her lira that they agreed to her request. By this time Linda was furious and the old lady was quiet.

It seemed to Ralph that there was something intrinsically comic and pathetic in their voyage through this city with an old lady in tow. Venice itself was old, with failing kidneys, clogged channels, a ghostly confection which was turning sour and gooey like one of its own ice creams. He was bitterly disappointed, as if his whole trip had been in vain. And now and again, too, he would feel dizzy. He had thought that his mind would fill like the tide with an abundance of fresh images but in fact all he saw around him was the imposed vision of the tourists: it was they who had written this play, this was their script and scenario, and Venice was responding to it. It was this cheap theatre that the people wanted, not his novels at all. They wanted these trashy silvery gondolas, lacking in style and substance. They wanted that gilt instead of gold.

After a while they entered the church mainly to escape from the heat. But it was full of tourists with cameras, and now and again there would be a flash of light out of the cool dimness. There were candles everywhere, some red, some white: and images of the Virgin Mary and of Christ. Ralph peered at Latin inscriptions and tried to decipher them. The altar looked beautiful but theatrical. Altogether he didn't like the church. It wasn't austere enough: the atmosphere wasn't at all holy. Though it was a huge building, in its colour and pageantry it was too gaudy, too altogether garish. The images in it didn't seem to be all that different from those in the souvenir shop. Christianity itself was a set of souvenirs. The thought came to him that the walls needed a good coat of paint and he smiled. How could a saint be buried under these cheap stones?

"I don't believe it," said his mother-in-law again.

"Believe what?" said Linda.

"That St Mark is buried here. I must read my Bible again."

"I don't think it will tell you that in the Bible," said Ralph.

"Come on," said Linda abruptly and they re-entered the fierce sunlight which hit them with harsh strokes. They sat down on the hot steps on which they had sat recently. The large woman was gone. Linda took from her handbag the small vase which was the only thing that she had bought. A girl who had taken the place of the big woman smiled and gazed longingly at the vase. Their mother was prepared to speak to her but the girl made signs that she couldn't understand English.

To think that this was Venice, Ralph thought, gazing distastefully at the vase. Was everything then a deceit, cheap theatre, when you came right down to it? Venice appeared to him like a decayed music hall he had once seen in Wales. The actors had passed through it and had gone, leaving a legend behind them that was essentially false. He felt tremendous sorrow, grief, as he shifted his bottom on the hot stone. Was he himself as hollow as this city? An old finished prima donna.

Impatiently Linda said, "I think we should make our way to the ship." And so they retraced their footsteps, climbing and ascending steps, beaten upon by the pitiless sun. Nearer the ship they sat down on a bench and Linda took from her handbag the only postcard she had bought. It showed gold-encrusted gondolas sailing on green canals.

She addressed it to Violet who was staying next door and wrote carefully. "We're in Venice today. Very hot, very nice. You should have seen the church." When she had finished she smiled ironically at Ralph.

They sat and watched the white ship. It would be their cool saviour taking them away from the inferno of Venice.

While they were in Porec they also visited other places. One was Pula, the town at whose airport they had landed on their arrival, and the other was Portojua with its big caves. Otherwise they rested a lot of the time, keeping themselves out of the devouring sun which fed on tourists like a large golden bristling animal. Ralph began to think of himself as a delicate white Greek, aloof and distant, while Linda grew more and more impatient with him. She herself was gregarious, impulsive, generous. He on the other hand was the eternal watcher, the reporter, the spectator on the edge of things. She had far more life than he had, far more energy. He compensated for his lack of life by creating worlds which were often hesitant and often cold.

The day they went to Pula it was almost unbearably hot. The bus was like a burning cage and the driver didn't leave the door open as they travelled. They talked to a woman whose husband had been taken to hospital with a heart attack. "They have been very kind to him," she said. But it was odd to think of her having domestic trouble in a distant land like this.

When they got off the bus they wandered down to the market. Linda loved markets, they suited her gipsy transient nature; their colours, their trinkets, their suits and dresses hung out in the open air on rails, attracted her. She loved the jewellery, the woman applying lipstick to her lips at her stall.

After the market they went into the shops. All around them

95

were the high-buttocked tourists with their cameras strung about their necks. They looked so confident, so charged with the wine of sex, the girls with flaring breasts and bottoms tight in jeans. This was what nature should be like, flowering, blossoming, fruits of the transient days. Ralph felt his own white Greekness being devoured, as if he were going mad with love of all these temporary beings. They were almost holy, while his mother-in-law was old and veined with ancient rivers steadily failing in her legs. Linda too was beautiful in that extraordinary glitter and light.

Eventually they stopped at the Roman amphitheatre which was larger than any Ralph had ever seen before. It was roofless, with stone seats. It was a vast empty vase of stone which hoarded the frightening power of the sun. As he sat inside it he thought of the women with their glowing animal eyes, the emperor turning his thumb down, the gladiators with throbbing muscles and swords and nets, the calm-eyed lions and lionesses blinking as they emerged from the darkness of the stalls. There had been days of real life and real death in this ring. In the same way as the rabbit cowers before the weasel, before the dancing stoat, in its advancing playful iron rings of necessity, so too had the slaves watched the lions come. He felt as if he was being slowly broken, hammered into cheap stucco.

"Did you read the story in the guide book?" he asked Linda.

"What about?"

"Why there is no roof on the amphitheatre."

"And why isn't there?"

"It is said that the fairies were building it and the cock crew at dawn and so they had to leave. So they never finished it."

"That's a beautiful story," said Linda. She imagined the fairies with their tiny hammers, and then the feared dawn with its clouds of red ore appearing over the horizon.

Ralph thought of the Englishman and the Englishwoman they had met. He had been a clerk in the Civil Service and he had just had a major operation and was returning to one. He used to umpire cricket matches on green Sundays in southern England. In the middle of the amphitheatre this Civil Servant stood, his thumb pointing down at the amateurish green, tall and stricken. Then he was locked into an iron cage and was feverishly jotting down the numbers of lions and lionesses that were cantering into the arena. Would anyone listen to the fair judgement of an umpire here? In that world, Roman and remorseless, there had perhaps been no referees, there was only the bloodstained emperor, the cries of the hungry plebs avid for sensation. The light burned people to death, they were meshed in shadows.

His mother-in-law was looking for a toilet again but there was none. There was no one here but Japanese, Germans, Frenchmen, strolling about in the amphitheatre, training their cameras on it. The sun beat on Ralph's head like a hammer. He moved in a languor of heat. The umpire stood in the centre of the amphi-theatre in his white coat like a surgeon's, and the golden-eyed lions leaped towards him. He was counting them off in a little book he held in his hand and they slunk towards him, their jaws ravening. They had come from Africa, they had eaten their way through cemeteries on their journey towards Rome, towards Pula. He looked at Linda, bewildered and amazed. It was as if her body, his own, that of her mother, were eatable, bones being torn from the flesh, devoured by the lions, sleepy and powerful. He swayed in the middle of the arena. Lights and flame flashed in front of his eyes as if he were watching a continuous television set. The light itself was an animal and the people its prey. Cruel Roman heads glared out of the stone among the roses. Here it was that true tragedy had begun and flowered, in the countries of hot climates, not in the doubtful double countries of the cold and the ice.

Linda looked radiant. She was so kind to animals, to people, so aware of their pain. Did she not see to what kind of land they had come? The quick bright sudden thrust, the world of the animals, man as a body not a spirit (only in the cold countries was man a cold white spirit, a ghost). Ralph's shirt hung sweatily on him, like a becalmed sail. He was pouring with sweat, a waterfall of hot moist perspiration. Linda looked calm and radiant in her white blouse. Ralph passed his hand across his brow, mopping the sweat away. The sky above the roofless amphitheatre was a cloudless blue without any shadow of thought on it. It was a world without reflection, brutal and barbarous. He couldn't write in a place like this. It would disable him with its ferocious heat and light. It demanded instant reflexes, of terror, fear, lust. There was no shelter, no hiding place. It did not compose long meandering reflective narratives. Its morality was that of this pitiless light. The sun was a golden ball which bounced from stone.

"Come on," he said suddenly. Did they not see what he saw, could they not see it? Was he going mad? It was as if the sun was flaying him, tearing strips from his flesh, burning his spirit, cauterizing it. They were like ghosts in this inferno.

"Is something wrong?" said Linda.

"No. Nothing. It's just the . . . heat." But it was worse than the heat, it was a vision of the ultimate animal world. He saw the Japanese, the Germans, the Frenchmen turning on each other, eating each other, mounting each other. There was a flagrant riot of copulating flesh while the wounded dying clerk sat at his tall desk counting. And the sleepy eyes of the lions emerged out of the darkness like jewels. Like yellow jewels.

His whole body was a dying arena of sweat, he was shaking and trembling. He put his hand in his pocket and popped a red pill in his mouth. And the Roman stony face smiled at him for taking it. He was hiding from the terror of real life, from the rending jaws, the bloodied teeth. The amphitheatre was a calm ship in the middle of a burning ocean, stone sails set. And the women in the front seats had glittering eyes as they watched the gladiator with the spidery net and the massive throbbing parts. Their dresses were a pure white avid flame.

"Are you all right?" said Linda.

"I'm fine," said Ralph again. They left the amphitheatre and made their way towards the bus. It was the same hot cage as before, and they had to wait, door shut, till two German girls who had got lost returned. "Move, move," said Ralph under his breath to the driver, for he was almost unable to breathe. There was not a whisper of a breeze. The seats under the open roof at the back had all been taken, the leather of the others was on fire.

This was one of the circles of hell.

"Did you notice," said Linda, "as we were coming to Pula that they cultivate everything. Every little part of land they cultivate. And the vines, they have so many vines."

"Yes," said Ralph, recalling the cars drawn up among the vine fields. "They work very hard. No question about it."

"Well, I didn't like Palma much," said his mother-in-law. Palma? Where was Palma? Was there an actual place called Palma? She would go home and talk about that hot day in the amphitheatre in Palma. Linda smiled at him and he smiled back. His mother-in-law was busy changing the terminology of the country in which they were. She sometimes called it Czecho-slovakia.

Suddenly she said, "I think he had cancer."

"Who?" said Linda.

"The man from Scotland we met the other day."

"From England," said Linda. "He was from England."

"Wherever he was from he had cancer. He can't deceive me. I've seen people like that before. His wife is hiding it from him but he has cancer." And her face looked inflexible.

The two German girls still hadn't come. And the bus moved off in search of them, slowly, bearing its freight of heat.

Ralph put his hand in his pocket to see if his passport was there but remembered that Linda had it locked in her case in the hotel.

She seemed to him to be much younger than he was. She could, unlike him, have lived in this hard immediate light.

"That was a quaint story about the roof of the amphitheatre," said Linda.

"Yes, wasn't it?" He imagined the fairies preparing to slide the roof into place like the tombstone on top of the Englishman who was going to have the operation: and the dawn rose red over Istria and over the sea, and the cock crew, with its angry red comb, and the fairies had to flee back to wherever they had come from.

"Fairies," said his mother-in-law. "No such thing. They used to talk about fairies, but back of my hand to them."

"There are more things in heaven and earth," said Linda. "Witches, fairies. There may be."

"Not unless Mary Macinnes is a witch," said her mother. "She's the only witch I've seen."

Linda laughed. Mary Macinnes was an old lady of eighty who lived by herself in a huge white house and read Ouspensky. She was much interested in religion, the more arcane the better.

The two German girls were found, and the bus headed out for the country. There was a flutter of air from the roof. The iron cage cooled: they had left the arena.

Unlike the colosseum the caves at Portojua were very cold, after the heat of the upper world. In a large straggling crowd they followed their guide whose name was Nino, a young Italian. He led them towards a train which would take them down into the caves. On the platform was a woman in a green cape who made

99

sure that they were safely in their seats before the train left. It rocked from side to side and though they instinctively bent their heads to prevent themselves being hit by the stone above them it was certain that clearance had been allowed for. All the time an eerie icy air blew coldly towards them. It was like being in the centre of a chilly womb, deep in the middle of the earth. Linda's mother was hanging on desperately, frightened out of her wits. After what seemed quite a long time the train came to a stop and they saw another woman, also in a green cloak, waiting for them. She looked impersonal, professionally remote, harsh. She shouted at a passenger in a foreign accent which sounded machine-like, "Don't get off till train stops." It was as if she belonged to this eerie underground world, as if she never rose to the sunny world above.

They helped their mother out of the train and found themselves standing in a vast space with people of all nationalities milling around them.

"Where is the guide," said Ralph in a panic.

"Look," said Linda, "there's a notice."

She felt quite relaxed and in charge of the other two. The notice stated that English-speaking people should follow an English-speaking guide, Germans a German-speaking one and so on. Linda drew the other two into the appropriate queue.

Before they set off the guide told them a little about the caves. Ralph hardly listened, and neither did his mother-in-law. She was clutching Linda's arm with the desperation of death. They followed the guide upwards and along a wooden path which here and there was wet and slippery with melting ice. Directly in front of them was a fair-haired woman, probably German, leading a fair-haired little girl, a small duplicate of herself. Their mother grasped the railing with fear and nervousness. Ralph noticed on his left-hand side a worm-like pattern of brown clay. There were stalagmites — or were they stalactites? — of a pink coral colour.

All around him he could see fantastic images, as in an illustrated book of ice. There were gnomes shaped from ice, the icy faces of old men and old women, and what looked like two chess players facing each other and immersed in an icy game, with icy pawns and icy bishops. Below the wooden path he sensed chasms of water while to all sides of him there were these crazy obsessed shapes as if they had once been real warm-blooded people on which an Ice Age had unexpectedly descended. Stalagmites — stalactites?? hung their sharp swords. The lights turned the icy columns into an enchanted autumn wood.

It was a world such as he had never seen before and he was afraid of it. Sweat broke out on his body though the caves were icy cold. It seemed to him too that it was a world he had inhabited before, symbolically, a book of icy characters frozen perpetually, unable to come to life, to move. It would need a huge effort of the imagination to fill them with life and animation. They were distant, cold, bizarre, locked in their own world. He passed his hand across his brow to wipe the sweat away. He looked at Linda but she seemed to be quite calm, gazing around her with interest. His mother-in-law was hanging on to the railing for dear life muttering to herself what might have been a prayer. He imagined misers counting their icy coins and transported to a perpetual hell. He shivered suddenly in the draught of cold wind. He thought, If one got lost here, if one were separated from the others, one would never find one's way again back to the warm circle, the central human fire. It was like hell itself except that it was bitterly cold. The guards in their infernal green — symbols of nature gone poisonous — had unsettled him with their quaint mechanical English: they were like robots in the service of an unknown god. He felt dizzy, unstable. Images wavered in front of him, with faces of conscious repellent evil. Even his mother's face looked evil, witchlike.

"It's beautiful," breathed Linda. "So intricate."

He didn't answer. He didn't think of it at all as beautiful. It was as if the crazy images in his mind had become objectified in this place in a bizarre surrealistic fashion. He was surrounded by his own imperfect creations, getting on with their own business, not caring about him, and not even looking at him. It was as if he was in a morgue. The script of his life unrolled before him. The daggers of ice pointing downwards were smooth and shiny. Faces of old women peered cunningly from the centre of the pink involuted forest.

"In the middle of the wood." In the enchanted autumnal forest.

"Mother, are you all right?" said Linda.

"No I'm not. I want to get out of here."

"It won't be long now," said Linda.

This is the end, thought Ralph, this is what we have always been heading towards, this place with its frozen music, this air of the last cold. He felt angry with himself for being so afraid. After all, all the others there, apart from his mother, seemed to be enjoying themselves. He looked down into the icy chasm below and drew back. He could hear the guide talking in the distance but couldn't make out what he was saying, the chatter of alien water.

It seemed to him suddenly that he would never write again, and he felt a deep nameless sorrow. These extraordinary rounded shapes like sleeping animals, this land of gnomes, icy and bearded, was a world that he had not invented, and it belonged to a foreign frozen continent utterly beyond the power of the mind. These were not the friendly sculptures of Greece. He couldn't control it. It had its own inner music which did not belong to him. What infinite power it would need to set it in motion, like a frozen roundabout. He didn't have the energy, the enthusiasm.

His mother-in-law was still muttering to herself, and when he spoke to her she didn't answer. He was sure that she was uttering fragments of the Bible like spells: she was talking about the valley of death, green pastures. Normally he would have winked to Linda as if to say, "Listen to her". But he didn't have any inclination to do so: he envied her in fact her simple faith. What was she seeing, thinking about? If one needed a translator to talk to the Yugoslavs, how much more did he need a translator to interpret her? Fragile and frail, she walked through the Valley of Darkness clutching the wooden rail, looking down at her feet lest she should slip on the wooden steps. Death was close to her, but as for him it was panic, darkness, that enveloped him. Like the brown worm the queue unwound itself along. Like a bandage.

And then they were back in the middle of the vast space again. And on the platform were the eerie guards in their green cloaks. How desperately he longed for the heat, the light, for the upper world above. He had a hunger for the sun which illuminated the earth, made art possible.

They took their seats on the train. As it rocked along Ralph remembered the Curtain which, just like any other curtain, hung over an overarching rock down which droplets of water fell. It was white almost to the edge, but the edge itself was brown with shades of orange and red. The Curtain wavered in front of his mind like an after-image. And alongside it there appeared frozen trees, cherry trees of ice: frozen kettles that would never boil: a shape like a cock crowing silently out of the desert of ice.

The air warmed a little as they rocketed along swaying from side to side. His mother was silent, her lips tightly locked together. Linda as usual was gazng around her with her free open stare. The train came to a halt and they climbed towards the hot dazzling sun. Then they were out of the caves completely and near a restaurant and souvenir shop.

"What about a coffee?" said Ralph brightly.

They went into the restaurant and drank their coffees and waited. It would be another half hour before the bus would leave.

"Never again," said his mother.

"You didn't like it," said Linda.

"Never again," she repeated.

"What about you, Ralph?"

"Not much."

He relished the movement around him, the heat on his head and arms and hands, the women spooning ice cream into the mouths of their children. But he was sweating furiously and he had to wipe his face over and over. It was as if he was melting. The strange terrible tiredness that was like a weight on him: these shapes that would not move: these characters that would not obey him but sat at their cold chess games: the barren script, becalmed drama: all these oppressed him.

"I thought it was beautiful," said Linda.

As they walked to the bus her mother clung to Linda as she had clung to the railing. They saw their guide in front of them with two girls, laughing and joking.

"He should have been with us," said his mother-in-law furiously. "He just disappeared. I've a good mind to report him."

The day they were to leave they were up early. In fact Ralph had been counting the hours till their departure, as was his mother-in-law. This was an undecipherable land, strange and alien. The faces presented to them were masks though behind them must seethe the common emotions, griefs and joys. Ralph felt that he was returning home in complete ignorance. The foreign advertisements glared out at them from the rain that was falling. There seemed to be a scarcity of vowels in the names of the places they passed.

After they had been driven by bus to the airport they joined the queue at the duty-free shop.

"I'll take apricot brandy, and cigarettes of course," said his mother-in-law.

A man who said he came from Glasgow told them when the plane would be leaving: it had been slightly delayed but it would leave shortly, he assured them. It seemed to Ralph that he was trying to calm himself as much as them.

They crossed the tarmac in driving rain and ascended the steep steps. After they had climbed from the airport a stewardess asked the man from Glasgow for his ticket. He searched his pockets for what seemed to be hours before he found it in his back pocket. It was crumpled up like a sweaty pound note.

"Lucky for you I found it, hen," he said to the stewardess who smiled thinly. The carelessness of it, thought Ralph, and asked Linda if she had the tickets in her handbag. It was the fifth time since he had entered the plane.

Linda pointed the Alps out to her mother again. The latter recalled the teacher who had told her about them. "In those days," she said, "we had to bring a kettle to school for our dinner. Imagine that."

So that was Yugoslavia. Have I been changed in any way, thought Ralph. No, he considered. It had all been a mystery, impenetrable and closed, though the sun shone openly every day. It was a different and unknowable book. He had stared into the whiteness without shadow.

When the plane landed at Glasgow it was obvious that it had been raining there too, for the ground was green and damp. They walked from the plane into a chilly wind and stood watching their revolving cases.

Then they went to the taxi rank. The driver of their taxi helped them with their cases: the three of them looked tanned and prosperous and rich in story. Glasgow though wet and dismal seemed more solid than Porec, its tenements bigger and dirtier yet more spacious. There it was the sun that had cracked walls, here it was the rain.

The driver called the old lady "hen". He said he couldn't

believe that she was eighty and indeed she looked younger, and almost black with the sun. He unloaded their cases for them at the railway station and the old lady insisted on giving him an extra pound.

"Thanks, hen," he said, and bowed to her as if she were a queen. She blushed with pleasure. As they waited for the train Ralph rushed over to the bookstalls and bought armfuls of magazines, newspapers, and read feverishly as if he were starving.

The train snaked north and he could see his mother-in-law visibly relaxing. Yugoslavia fell away from her like a cloak. This was her own land, reliable, solid, familiar, and reassuringly wet. Birds flew about with drenched wings. Cows grazed. The rivers teemed with water and foam.

Later they all sat in Violet's living room while their mother told her of their journey.

"The airport was called Palma but you should have seen their food. It was mishmash, and spam. You wouldn't have given it to a mouse, and they had no public toilets. They were very strange people. I think they're very close to the Russians: they thought we were spies. No, I didn't like Czechoslovakia at all. You can keep it for me, back of my hand to it." Now and again she would go out into her garden and touch a rosebush, taking possession again. She would stand in the kitchen and touch a real loaf with wonderment. The holiday had been a dream to her. "And these caves," she said, "they were like hell itself. I never thought I would come out alive and as for Venice you wouldn't think anything of it. It was just shops with dolls and ships in them."

"Do you think she might visit Czechoslovakia again," said Ralph smiling to Linda.

"I'm warning you," said Linda smiling back.

"And there was one waiter there," said his mother-in-law. "Looked like Calum Gray. And a big square woman. Thighs like Mrs Simpson.

"And there was a man with a gun at Palma. I thought he was going to shoot us." As he listened to his mother-in-law it was as if they had been in two different countries. Yet what difference did it make? Yugoslavia, Czechoslovakia: Pula, Palma. Reality was what the tourists made of it. He remembered the day they had visited Pula and when he had shut his eyes kaleidoscopic images had wheeled in front of him on a perpetually changing screen. Again he felt the bone-tiredness and wished to go to bed but his mother-in-law was holding court, home at last with her own household gods. The roses in the garden seemed threatening to him and the grass so tall it might devour him at any moment. He had stared deeply at the meagreness and found himself without story or legend or narrative to defend himself with. He shook with fear.

Three

WHEN HE WOKE up he didn't know where he was, till the nurse spoke to him. She appeared out of a darkness which had been total.

"You're fine," she said, "fine." Her uniform crackled about him, and her round cheerful face was bent over him.

As he lay in the bed he began to shout and swear.

"I want to phone," he shouted. He tried to get out of bed but the nurse pushed him back.

"I'll bring you the phone," she said. The phone was wheeled across the floor of the ward. Patients stared at him gauntly but he didn't care. He dialled and heard the phone ringing in Linda's house; he thought of it as Linda's house, not his own. It rang and rang for a long time and then he heard Linda's voice.

"I want to see you at once," he shouted. "What are you trying to do to me? Who is there with you? I know there is someone there with you."

"There is no one here but mother," said Linda who sounded exhausted.

"You're lying," he shouted. "What's this place I'm in?"

"You're in hospital."

He grunted. "Come and see me at once."

"Do you know what the time is?"

"What? What did you say?"

"I said do you know what the time is. It's eleven o'clock at night."

"I don't care, I want you to come here at once."

He was frightened that she would never come again, that she had left him in this hospital, if hospital it was, in order to get rid of him. "You've got someone there," he shouted again. He knew that all the patients were glaring at him, that they were spying on him, but it didn't bother him. The man in the next bed was sitting up cradling his head in his hands and moaning to himself.

"If you don't come . . ." he shouted threateningly, and slammed the phone down. The same nurse who had brought it wheeled it away again. There was a lot of noise in the ward. Beds were being pushed across the floor making a screeching noise. Trolleys too were shifted. It seemed to him that the nurses were being deliberately noisy, that they could have lifted the beds, the trolleys. They didn't smile but looked at him in a hostile manner.

He felt that he must watch everything that happened around him very closely, and make a mental note of it. He lay in his bed for a while seething and then became so angry that he shouted for the phone again. The nurse unsmilingly brought it and he shouted again at Linda,

"I suppose you've taken the bug out of the car. That was evidence, you know. Who's been working with you. Is it someone who knows how to treat tapes? It must be. You must have met someone who knows about these things."

"I don't know what you're talking about."

"That night we went for a walk I noticed that you kept away from the river so that the bug would catch what I was saying clearly. Where did you wear it or did you carry it in your handbag? Why did you take your handbag with you when you went for a walk?"

"You know I always carry my handbag."

"Oh, I know you. You want my money. Why did you tear my telephone book? Why did you agree to marry me? That's what I want to know."

He could hardly hear Linda's voice, it was so faint and tired. And then it occurred to him that she wasn't in the house at all, she was in the house of her fellow conspirator, the man who had fixed the tapes for her. Or she might even be in a room in this very hospital, laughing at him. There was something wrong with the phone. Her voice was very far away.

"You can't deceive me," he shouted. "I'll tell you that. I'm brighter than you. I can work it all out. This isn't a real hospital. If it was a real hospital why is there so much noise? A hospital is supposed to be quiet."

There was a long silence at the other end of the line. "Are you consulting your friend," he shouted. "And what are you doing to my books and manuscripts? You have plenty of time now to mess everything up. You were always jealous."

He thought he heard the sound of weeping, but that of course was only a pretence, and he continued implacably to berate her. Her trickery was endless. It was quite clear to him that she had employed someone who knew about electronic devices. Certainly she had a lover. He pictured him as fat and heavy, a slow depraved smiling sexual man, the image of the taxi driver.

He slammed the phone down again lest she should have the satisfaction of cutting him off. The nurse wheeled it away again. The man in the next bed was still clutching his head and moaning. He was rocking with pain.

His own anger was uncontrollable. He nearly asked the nurse for the phone again but decided not to do so. Another nurse came and patted his pillow and handed him some yellow pills. He swallowed them quickly and lay in his bed thinking. All around him were enemies, he was sure of that. The nurses were only disguised as nurses, the patients weren't real patients. It was quite hopeless. Who would listen to his story, who would believe that Linda was what she was? He would keep silent and watch. There was no one here he could talk to.

His eyes closed and he fell asleep.

When he woke in the morning it seemed to him that he felt much better. A friend of his, a teacher, whom he had asked for without remembering it, and whom Linda had asked to come and see him, arrived with newspapers. He himself had been ill in this very hospital but had recovered. He inquired how he felt, while the sun poured into the ward, among the vases with their flowers, the white beds, the polished floor.

"Better," he said. "But there's one thing I would like you to do for me. I should like you to tell my lawyer to come and see me. I don't trust my wife. She wants to destroy me."

"I'm sure that's not true," said his friend.

"I know her better than you." For some reason this was the only person he trusted though he couldn't understand when he had asked for him.

They talked for a while. His friend was a teacher in a High School. He told him how a woman had come to the school with a knife ready to attack a young teacher who had just started in the school.

"That didn't happen in the old days," he said. "But then you're lucky. You're a writer, you can do what you want to do."

Ralph stared at him as if he were a visitor from another world. Everyone thought that he did nothing, that his writing was a hobby, and he had long given up the intention of convincing them otherwise.

After his friend had gone he tried to read the *Scotsman* but found that he couldn't concentrate. He took twenty minutes to read one column. He almost wept with frustration, he who had read so rapidly and easily in the past. It must be the drugs, he thought, it must be the drugs. Once I finish with the drugs I will be as I always was. But he couldn't be sure that he would ever be again as he had once been. He felt elegiac, posthumous.

To live without books, that would be impossible. For what else was there? Only the random flashes of chance, only this ward of so-called nurses, with their bedpans and their thermometers. In a fury he threw the *Scotsman* away from him to the floor. A man who was making his way slowly to the bathroom clutching his dressing-gown about him, and whose face was dead white, bent and picked it up.

"Can I borrow it?" he said.

"If you like," said Ralph. Patients walked about the ward, but didn't come to speak to him. It was of course part of the conspiracy: they wished to isolate him. There was probably nothing wrong with that white-faced man. He searched around in his locker and found cigarettes and matches. There were also sweets and fruit that Linda had probably left him and some loose money: he counted the money very carefully. It came to four pounds ten pence. There were three oranges, and two apples and four bananas. His silk dressing-gown was in there as well and his slippers.

The doctor came into the ward followed like an amiable shark by a shoal of nurses. He was a big rather fat sunny man and when he stopped at Ralph's bed he said, "Feeling better?"

"Can I have a cigarette?" said Ralph.

"Of course," said the doctor. Ralph took a cigarette from the packet and put it in his mouth and before he could light it the doctor leaned forward and lit it for him. However in his hurry to light the match the doctor let it fall from his hand on to the pillow, leaving a mark there, before Ralph could put it out. He stared at the doctor and the mark with hatred. So this was another of their tricks. They would say that he had lit a cigarette contrary to regulations and burned the pillow. Then they would put him in a mental home,

"Sorry about that," said the doctor. "It just shows you shouldn't be a doctor and smoke." The nurses smiled as if the doctor had made a huge joke. They would hold the burn on the pillow against him, he knew that.

"Now then," said the doctor jovially. "Listen carefully. I'm going to tell you a little story and I want you to answer some questions afterwards. Are you listening carefully? Good. All right then. Once upon a time there was a Mr Brown and he lived at 42 Grant Street. He had a sister called Julia who often visited him. His sister was older than him by four years and she had a family of three sons and a daughter. She usually brought them with her as she worked in a factory making tyres. She travelled by bus to see him and on this particular day which was a Monday she arrived. She found him watching television. . . ." He stopped as if bored with his own story. Then he said casually.

"What was the sister's name?"

"Julia."

"Very good. How did she come to visit him?"

"By bus."

"How many children did she have?"

"Three sons and a daughter."

"What was Mr Brown's address?"

"42 Grant Street."

"Very good indeed," said the doctor. "Especially after all these drugs. Now, you remember that address. I might ask you about it again."

He moved on, humming, accompanied by his coterie of adoring nurses. Ralph stared at the mark on the pillow and then after a while turned the pillow over so that the mark could not be seen. He had to watch what he was doing all the time. That wasn't a particularly good story, in fact it wasn't a story at all, it was a meagre plotless series of facts. What did the doctor think he was? An idiot? Suddenly he was filled with a deep grief. There was that doctor who had a job which he could do every day, a comfortable routine. And he himself was without one. Even the nurses had jobs. What a marvellous thing it was to have a job that one could do, where one didn't have to create afresh every day, invent plots, startling denouements. The ordinary world was richer, safer, than he had thought. But then he considered that the doctor wasn't a real doctor nor the nurses real nurses. After all, would a real doctor be so careless as to drop a match on a pillow or even allow him to smoke? Yet the doctor moved with such assurance, as if the ward belonged to him, the stethoscope dangling from his pocket. And he himself couldn't even concentrate on reading. Reading had been his whole life, he couldn't live without it. Tears came to his eyes as he thought of the books that he would never read again, as he thought that never again would he hear the inner hum of his mind.

A nurse came and patted his pillow and another one wheeled a trolley towards his bed in preparation for giving him a meal. For the first time, as the trolley squeaked towards him, he examined it carefully. There were only two wheels on it, two of the legs had no wheels at all. So that was why it screeched and squeaked. That was another of their tricks. That nurse had definitely wanted him to see the trolley and to see that it only had two wheels on it. It was obviously intended to make him mad, to disorientate him. He wanted to say something to the nurse about the trolley but decided not to. If he commented on things like that, they would definitely think him mad, they would tell others about his odd questions. And again why was the name of the street in the doctor's story called Grant Street? In the novel he had been working on there was a character called Grant. He had taken the name from the telephone book which had been mysteriously torn. The trickery went further back than he had thought. They were all in the plot, not only Linda but the doctor and the nurses. Even the questions had been thought out in advance. There was a beautiful symmetry in the whole business. Maybe his mother-in-law was in the plot too. She didn't like him reading all the time. She would know doctors and nurses. Perhaps there was a secret union such that they looked after each other. If someone was to be got rid of, then the mafia of doctors and nurses would gather together like a mysterious clan and do it. Who checked on them? Nobody that he knew of. People like him could be eliminated by such a mafia, members of the secret union.

He felt entirely at peace as the nurse brought food to him. There was no way in which he could outwit these people except by silence. They expected him to ask questions which would indicate that he was mad, but he would not satisfy them. He would remain buried in his deep silence, he would use exile and cunning against them, for he was on his own, there was no one to help him. And of course Linda was behind it all, like a spider. He imagined her with her fat secret lover drinking wine somewhere and talking about him, drawing the web tighter and tighter, inventing new ideas to drive him mad. Her lover must be that taxi driver. All that story about being a Catholic and having a wife and children was an invention. He and Linda and his mother-in-law were laughing behind his back even now, thinking how naive he had been while this immense plot had been spun round him. What he admired almost professionally was the perfection of the detail. They hadn't forgotten about the trolley. Of course they envied him, all of them, that was why they had decided to play this game on him. They had thought him an élitist and had isolated him. They had resented his ability to sustain himself on his own.

Perhaps that was why Linda had chosen Yugoslavia. She must have known that there would be no English language papers. It was she who had suggested that he hand over all his newspapers and magazines to the people in the hotel. The whole plot was a very intricate one, calculated precisely to deceive him. Every hero must be attacked at his weakest point and his weakness had been his capacity for creating fables, plots, while despising other people. He stared at a vase, blinded by the beauty of it all. Click after click as of the machinery in a safe was heard, elegant, complicated yet sublimely simple. All this had started a long time ago while he had been involved in writing, innocent, naive. Even the visit to the caves, to the colosseum, had been part of it, designed to drive him mad with images of hell and the underground, Orpheus and the icy Eurydice.

The trees outside the window swayed gently in the breeze. There was a world outside, which he would never taste again. It was heartbreakingly beautiful with its blossoms and its innocent rivers and streams. They had certainly locked him in, tricked him brilliantly. How had he survived? They wouldn't have liked that. On the other hand perhaps they hadn't wanted him to kill himself, they had wanted him to suffer. It would be too simple, too easy, to let him kill himself, that would be far too easy an exit. They had saved him for their own deep purposes. And then again they could say, How could we have destroyed him if we saved him from the death he tried to inflict on himself? Oh, they were clever, so clever, there was nothing that they hadn't thought about. They had wanted him to suffer while at the same time they were showing the outer world their concern for him. Even the nurses hated him, he could see that. And the doctor had been laughing at him as he strutted about in his smooth pompous manner, inventing such a silly story, as if it were a parody of one of his novels.

He ate his food quietly, all the time staring at the trolley as if it were an exhibit from a crime of unimaginable subtlety. And had his mother-in-law been deliberately confusing him with her talk about Palma? Was that a test and was she, too, more subtle than he had thought? He had thought her stupid when in fact she was very clever, indeed one of the instruments of the story. And in any case she hated him and hadn't wanted him to marry her daughter.

He ate as best he could. No, he wouldn't starve himself, not for anybody. He would survive if he kept quiet, if he watched, if he didn't speak. They would not catch him by his speech. Silence was his only weapon, he, the hero, who was being systematically and shrewdly destroyed.

Somewhere in the next ward he could hear the hum of a hoover and remembered the woman dressed in blue who had passed through his own ward earlier on. She was another of the happy workers, ensconced in her undemanding job, while he lay there and thought and suffered. She belonged to a world which he could never enter again, the mafia had made sure of that. Even if he confessed his pride, it would do him no good now. There was no appeal from this tribunal. But he would not give in, he was too used to subtleties of plot to be deceived easily. He was a reader of conspiracies. They had picked the wrong man this time. They would know that they were dealing with a real brain even though it was half paralysed by drugs.

He looked again at the pillow and found that the burnt mark was uppermost. The nurse must have done that when she was bringing him his food. There was nothing that they weren't capable of. There she was standing over by the oxygen machine looking so innocent, so crisp, in her uniform, gazing candidly around the ward, as if it were her own territory. Nurses, he now realized, had an infinite capacity for evil and the power to use it. They could be sadists, their patients were helpless in their hands. They had a terrible desire for power, as his mother-in-law had: they pushed their helpless patients about, pummelling their beds, making them get up in the middle of the night. Their resentful minds burned with a dim yet powerful light.

He took his dressing-gown from the locker and put it on. Then he padded to the bathroom. The white-faced man was standing at the basin washing his face. Ralph looked into the mirror and saw the man staring at him. It seemed to him that the man was mad and would attack him, and so he went into the cubicle and sat down on the seat. As he sat there he noticed that there were yellow strokes of paint on the wall. It looked as if someone had started to paint the cubicle and then had stopped. The strokes however were not in any order, they were like a crazy scrawl of yellow lightning, now here, now there. He stared at them for a long time, frightened, panic-stricken. When he came out of the cubicle the white-faced man was gone as if he had never been.

As he lay on the bed again he began to think of the nurses and then of the woman in Yugoslavia who had sat at the table next to them. She had said, Too much laughing, or words to that effect. She had of course been a German, possibly a Nazi. Nurses too were like Nazis: that was what he had been trying to get hold of. The Yugoslavs had fought against the Nazis but latterly had welcomed them to their country as tourists. They had the biggest cars, the finest and newest luggage. It was curious how they had sold their birthright in this way, accepted the thirty pieces of silver. And then he thought of the women dressed in black he had seen walking along the promenade, these women who had suffered so much in the war, who now walked in a treacherous sunshine. And finally he thought of the girl on the swing composing larger and larger arcs of flight as she soared towards the sky and in particular he thought of the young weeping boy who had been made fun of.

He had followed Linda about all the time in Yugoslavia, he had allowed her to do the leading, to take the decisions. He had been so tired, so exhausted. He had been stalled in his book and had welcomed the holiday. But the holiday had done him no good because he hadn't been able to read.

That night when she came to visit him she told him what had happened, as she nervously twisted and untwisted her fingers. She looked very pale but not yet as pale as he would have liked.

"They put you under the stomach pump. I don't know whether you realize it but you were swearing a lot when you came out of it and you wanted the phone all the time. Your language apparently was atrocious, which is odd. They had to give you the phone to quieten you down."

"What happened to me?" said Ralph in a distant cold voice but at the same time with a sort of pride.

"You ran into the wood. Into the middle of the wood. The taxi driver and I followed you. He was really very good, he could have left you and gone home to Glasgow but he said that he had seen something like this before. Anyway we followed you into the wood. I was going frantic. We couldn't find you at first and then we did, just in time. Another ten minutes, perhaps five minutes. . . . There was a very nice policeman and we walked you up and down, up and down."

"Five minutes," said Ralph with the same pride.

"That's right."

"I might as well tell you," said Ralph, "I think you're having an affair with that taxi driver. I was thinking about it, and he looks like the sort of person who knows about bugs. Anyway they're always in touch with their headquarters in these taxis."

"What are you talking about?"

"Bugs. He looks the mechanical type. Anyway, I don't believe he's a taxi driver and I don't believe he's married."

"Where on earth would I have met him?"

"I don't know. How do I know? How do people meet people?"

"Really," said Linda. "Do you realize you're putting me under a lot of strain? How do you like the hospital?"

"I don't like it at all. It's not a real hospital. They're always pushing and pulling furniture about. Beds, trolleys. And the trolleys don't have wheels on all the legs."

"What did you say?"

"Look at that one then. It's only got wheels on two legs."

"I see that. It's certainly odd. But they're all the same, as you can see."

"What?"

"The trolleys are all the same. Have a look."

And when he did look he saw that they were indeed all the same. It wasn't just his trolley that had wheels on two legs only. But he was determined to continue.

"And another thing they've got streaks of yellow paint on the lavatory cubicle. As if someone had started and not bothered to finish. It's very odd."

118

Linda didn't say anything. Now and then she would pass her hand across her eyes. How cunning she was, pretending to be tired.

"I wish you would tell me more about this conspiracy," he said, "which I admire so much. I really do. I am a professional. I admire technique. Why don't you just come out into the open and tell me what you're doing and why you hate me so much."

"I don't hate you. I want you to get well. Surely you can see that I love you."

"Love!"

"Would I have rescued you if I hated you? Would I be coming to see you?"

"That's the cunning of it all. You want me to suffer."

"For what?"

"For living in my own world. I discovered that in Yugoslavia. I discovered your world. It was meagre. It frightened me. How can one live without an obsession such as art?"

"I don't know what you're talking about. What's meagre about it?"

"Nothing. What's the use? I've sent for my lawyer."

"Oh."

"That's right. I want to make a will. I never made a will before."

"If that's what you want."

He was watching her like a hawk but her expression didn't change.

"Yes. I might leave my money as a prize for a novel."

"You would need a lot for that, wouldn't you?"

"It's what I want to do."

"That's all right. If it will relieve your mind. I only want you well." But in spite of her protestations he sensed a falsity in what she was saying. He was filled with despair. How could you trust anyone in this world? What was going on behind the mask of smooth or wrinkled brows? He was in the middle of a spy story. Spy stories were very ordinary, they were around one all the time, they were about the double agents of the common day, the deaths and resurrections and betrayals. How could one even know who oneself was?

"I brought you fruit," she said.

"I've got fruit already," he said. "Look." And then he stared at his locker. "There were four bananas there. Now there are only three. And I didn't leave my slippers like that."

"You must have miscounted them."

"No I didn't. I definitely counted them." He felt very insecure as if behind his back all sorts of things were happening, nurses taking bananas when he was lying asleep or in the lavatory. And as for his slippers they must have shifted them too. But he must remain quiet and not say anything that would incriminate him or label him as mad.

"Go away," he said curtly. "I don't want you. I don't trust you. Go away."

She rose wearily to her feet.

"If that's what you want."

"That's what I want."

He watched her as she walked away from him and he thought she might be leaving him forever. He despised himself for being so dependent on her, for loving her. He nearly called her back but didn't. He wouldn't phone her either. He would show her that he didn't need her. He thought her bowed back, her weary walk, a beautiful .piece of acting. She disappeared through the open doorway and later he heard a car starting. He lay in his bed imagining her going home to a house where her fat lover awaited her and he was filled with despair. But also he had his pride. No, he wouldn't have anything more to do with her. When he got out of hospital he would leave her and find a flat for himself and live there forever reading his books if he could concentrate. But he was frightened of being left alone and he loved her so much.

He could hardly keep his eyes open. He knew that the nurses must be drugging him just before the visiting hour so that he couldn't question Linda closely. Oh, they were cunning: nothing they hadn't thought of. He shut his eyes and fell asleep.

When he woke up there was a harsh light falling about the ward. The nurses were in a frenzy of business shifting beds from one ward to another. In the bed next to him he saw the man who had been suffering a headache before. He was still clutching his head and rocking backwards and forwards. His eyes looked mad. He watched with a bleak understanding as he saw all the other beds being shifted out of the ward apart from his own and the sick man's. The latter gazed at him unseeingly. Why weren't they giving him anything for the pain? It must be deliberate on their part. Suddenly there were no nurses at all and the ward was quiet, apart from the moaning of the man in the next bed.

And then he saw the next part of the plot. It too was beautiful. The man was going to go off his head with the pain and attack him and they would say that they didn't realize he was so bad. It would be put down as an accident. The man's mad eyes glared through him, past him. In his striped pyjama jacket he was sitting up in bed, a mad tiger. Ralph felt more scared than he had ever done in his life before. The man was a maniac, he had been left alone with a maniac in the falling yellow empty light. What time was it? It must be about midnight. The ward felt eerie and deserted and there were no nurses to be seen. He wanted to speak to the man, to say, "I'm on your side. I hate these nurses too. They should have given you pain killers." But he couldn't bring himself to do so. His mouth was dry and he was lying there like a vulnerable effigy. He felt that the scene had been carefully staged. They were deliberately keeping the man in pain waiting to see what would happen. He himself was like a goat tethered in the harsh light waiting for the tiger to see him and attack. Yet why was he so frightened? Why should he be frightened of death, who had tried to kill himself. It was absurd, and yet he was. He didn't want to die, not here, not in this unintelligible place, which he couldn't control, without someone knowing, testifying, to what had happened. "Novelist attacked by patient." Everything of course would be covered: they always looked after their own.

In the distance as if from the kitchen he heard some music playing. 'Irene Good Night', it was. Who was playing a radio at this time of night? The man's head turned towards him like a jaguar's as if he was scenting a fresh disturbance. Of course they were deliberately doing it. This was a bare barren stage in its helpless yellow light like vomit, it was waiting for something to happen. The nurses were hiding and watching, perhaps laughing and chattering among themselves. They were waiting to see the result of their plan.

> Sometimes I live in the country
> sometimes I live in the town
> sometimes I take a great notion
> to jump into the river and drown . . .

Where had he heard that before? It was on the bus in Yugoslavia sung in a tinny Yugoslavian voice in English. The man was now staring helplessly down at the bed in a world of his own, abstract, cruel. And then he began to weep soundlessly, tears pouring down his face. As he did so he turned away from Ralph. The plot had failed, the tiger hadn't struck at all in the middle of the wood. He had escaped their machinations for one more night.

The following day at about eleven o'clock in the morning the lawyer came to visit him, young, brisk, energetic, clutching a briefcase.

"How are you, Ralph?" he said. "Feeling better?"

"Yes," said Ralph.

"Good, good. What we'll do is, I'll take your instructions and then bring you the will to sign. Okay?"

"Fine," said Ralph, "that will be fine."

"Okay then," said the lawyer again. He smiled as a nurse came and drew the curtains around the bed.

"I'll outwit her," said Ralph to himself. "I will leave her the money after all. I will do the unexpected." He thought that this was the best thing to do, to show his contempt, his self-sacrifice. To show a supreme irony. He felt better when he had thought of this plan, it was so unexpected, it had such an odd ending. It would make her ashamed. He felt fulfilled and heroic.

"I want to leave all my possessions to my wife," he said.

"And after that in the event of . . ." the lawyer paused, his pen in his hand.

"After her no one."

"I see."

How neat and tidy the lawyer was, how finely combed his hair, how well-shaved his cheeks, how efficient he was too. And how young.

"Well, there should be no problem about that," said the lawyer shutting his briefcase and looking around him with the same calm self-sufficient smile. What was he smiling at?

"I'll get this drafted out and in a day or two I'll come back." He stood up from his chair which was at the side of the bed. Then he glanced round him at the curtains and said, "Reminds me of amateur drama I used to take part in." Then he smiled again.

Of course, thought Ralph, he has no intention of making a will for me: he thinks I'm mad.

Ralph said hesitantly, "If anything happens to me . . ."

"Yes," said the lawyer quickly.

"Anything unusual. Keep your eye on the papers."

"Of course," said the lawyer. Was there a gleam of pity in his eyes?

"I mean," said Ralph, "you never know. Just keep your eyes peeled."

"Certainly, certainly." But Ralph knew that the lawyer wasn't listening to him, he was thinking of something else. Again he felt the piercing terrible despair.

"Right then," said the lawyer making his way through the involutions of the curtains which swelled around him like sails, like grave-clothes. He was ready to make his exit. Ralph wished to change his will again, to call him back, but the moment passed, and then he was gone, and the nurse was opening the curtains. The lawyer strode purposefully across the ward whose floor was as polished as himself. "I should phone," thought Ralph, "I should tell Linda what I've done. I should tell her about the irony of it all."

He rose from his bed and put on his dressing-gown and went to the bathroom. The white-faced man was there again staring into the mirror and again he went into the cubicle, locking the door in case his fellow patient attacked him. He was safe nowhere. Irony was no help in a place like this. It was lost on its residents. He glanced at the wall. More yellow strokes had been added in a crazy pattern. Fresh yellow strokes like lightning, like straws. Oh God, he was going out of his mind. Their inventions were endless, their skill in detail was phenomenal, far more brilliant than anything he had ever done. His mind felt dull beside theirs. He remembered Linda dancing on the boat, her vivid repertoire of theatre, creating dazzling props from the dullest of objects. Dancing, dancing. Of course she was masterminding this. How cruel they all were, they wouldn't leave him alone for a minute. The colours swam in front of his eyes like a kaleidoscope, as once on the bus ages ago in Pula. He rose heavily to his feet and walked back into the ward. The white-faced man had disappeared again. He tried to read the *Scotsman* that his friend had brought him but couldn't concentrate. He almost wept with rage and frustration.

As if from a great distance he heard the smart trim Nazi sister say to a nurse, "I could create a scene if I wanted to." Then she smiled and it seemed as if she was laughing at him. He hated her because she had made him stop smoking on account of the oxygen machine. He hated when she stopped at his bed. She spoke so sarcastically to him, she relished her power so much. She was adept at her work, writing reports assiduously with a quick light hand.

"You'll soon be back at your books," she said sarcastically to him. "Won't you?"

She didn't really know who he was, he wished he could tell her about himself, about his infinite superiority, but his mind was too dull. He wished he could dazzle her with his wit, but he could think of nothing to say. He hated her so much, she was so self-satisfied and smug. "You'll soon be out of here," she said laughing and her tone was infinitely menacing. She was one of the ones who would have been happy in concentration camps. Her horizons were limited, she was sharp, tart, aseptic. He looked for the ring on her hand and saw none. And yet she had told him that she was married. Alert, quick, she dominated the ward in charge of the other nurses, the auxiliaries. He saw a man in a neat blue suit speaking to her. He had dark hair, a red face as of someone who lived in the open air. But he was clearly a psychologist. Bitch, thought Ralph, diamond-hearted bitch, how I hate you. You were the one who was looking across to me the other night when I was talking to Linda. It was as if you were saying to her, Everything will be all right. The plan is going fine. Nazi bitch. And you told me you were married when you aren't. Otherwise where is your ring? You even told me about your daughter who was given a bad mark in English. What are you trying to do to me? In your white dress you look so clean, so pure, so careless of humanity, its stink and vomit. You hate humanity, that's quite clear, you wouldn't be so sarcastic otherwise. You should never have been a nurse at all, you are in the wrong profession.

He was told that he had an appointment with the visiting psychologist and was wheeled along in his dressing-gown by a large orderly. For a moment he was in the fresh air, just before he was deposited outside the psychologist's room. She was waiting for him behind a desk, her eyes intent and it seemed to him cold. He was of course quite sure that she was not a psychologist at all.

"And how are we today?" she said, with what he thought a false bonhomie.

"Better," he muttered.

"That's good," she said, studying him, and then some papers. "That's very good."

He sat upright, at attention before her like a small boy.

"I think we'll have to think about the next step, don't you?" She shuffled some papers like cards, letting the silence last for a long time, as if she expected him to say something. But he didn't answer. He must be quiet and watchful. Her hair was snow-white and her glasses glittered icily.

"I think it is time to transfer you," she said.

"The mental hospital?" he said.

"The Bayview," she said.

And he knew that the Bayview was a mental hospital. And he knew too that he would never leave it, he would be buried in it. He had seen too many programmes on television which showed how people had been falsely incarcerated for years in mental hospitals.

He stared down at the floor submissively.

"We will have to get you well, won't we?" she said.

Still he didn't speak. "It won't be long if everything goes according to plan," she said. "Are you quite happy to go there and get well?"

"I suppose so."

"Jolly good," she said. "I think you should go there tomorrow. I'll inform the sister."

"Yes," he said limply.

She scribbled on a piece of paper, intent, chilly, glacial.

"There is one thing," she said. "You shouldn't be making these worrying phone calls to your wife. She is under a great deal of pressure. And she loves you. Don't you believe she loves you?"

"No," he said.

"I see. Why then should she be visiting you? She has been to see me in tears."

"She brought it on herself," he muttered sullenly. "And in any case what is love?"

"I beg your pardon. What did you say?"

"Nothing."

"I see." She stared at him consideringly. He was quite sure that he was much brighter than this psychologist. For instance he had read Laing, he knew about mental illness and that it was caused

125

by environment. And he knew that he himself wasn't mentally ill. There were too many signs which indicated that his ideas and thoughts were correct. She must have had an amusing time dressing up as a psychologist seating herself behind this desk, watching him. There were some good actresses in this so-called hospital, no doubt about that. But then women enjoyed acting, they liked dressing up, trying on new clothes, jewellery. They were like wicked children.

"If there's nothing else then," she said in a raised questioning voice. He remained silent then got to his feet. He opened the door. Waiting there was the big man with the barrow. He sat in it, pulled the blanket over his legs, and was returned to his ward. After seeing the psychologist the ward was like home.

And to tell the truth he was frightened. What would a mental hospital be like? It would be full of violent madmen, some of whom might even attack him. If he wasn't mad now he soon would be. In his mind he had a picture of an old Victorian building with flaky walls, and pale manic toothless faces staring at him. All the inmates would be dressed in long nightgowns. Sometimes if he was lucky he might be wheeled out to the lawn which always fronted these places. And he would shiver in a cold wind, a blanket about his thin pale legs. He would need all his courage to survive. And he was quite sure that Linda wouldn't come to visit him at all: that was why the psychologist had mentioned the phone calls. She was preparing him for Linda's absence. The last move in the game had been played, now he would be abandoned. As he thought of this he began to shiver uncontrollably and clasped his body in his arms, staring up at the ceiling. He had been manoeuvred into a corner, he shouldn't have opened his mouth at that interview. He shouldn't have given that psychologist any chance of proving him mad.

The man in the next bed was clasping his head in his hands, the white-faced man was wandering about the ward from bed to bed but avoiding his. As he lay there he heard another patient being wheeled in and saw that it was the psychologist whom he had noticed earlier. He was now dressed in striped pyjamas and looked like any other patient. But only Ralph could see that he was really a psychologist set there to watch him. It could be no coincidence that he had appeared after he had seen the lady psychologist.

"Don't think I don't know who you are," he said to himself. "I know you all right. You can't deceive me."

This was hell nor was he out of it. These were the unfathomable glacial caves with the wind blowing through them. And instead of guards in green capes there were nurses dressed in blue and white. The tune of 'Irene Good Night' hummed in his mind. It went back to those days when he had done his National Service. It seemed to haunt his life.

"Jump into the river and drown." He remembered being in an army hospital with German measles and reading a book about the Middle Ages. That was his only experience of hospital previous to this. Even when he had been going down to Glasgow on that doomed train journey he had heard the tune beaten out on the wheels of the train louder and louder. And then again he had heard it in Yugoslavia, tinny, slightly wrong. He wouldn't be surprised if there was a nurse called Irene in the hospital at that very moment.

The horror he had felt when he had found his novel notes scattered in a drawer after he had left them lying neatly on top of his desk! They were all scribbled and scrawled on violently. And then he had found the telephone book torn in two. Who would have thought Linda had such strength in her? On the other hand it might have been the taxi driver who had torn it, he had the strength. The horror he had felt when objects began to change their places. Never before had there been such horror. Apart from now, when he waited to go to the Mental Home, who did not deserve to be in one but on the contrary could see as in a chess game the moves that were being made.

He looked over to his left and saw that the psychologist had put on the headphones which were above the bed. He wouldn't be listening to music, no, on the contrary he would be receiving his instructions, he would be keeping in touch with headquarters, with the nurses. He might even be listening to Linda's voice at that very moment. True, he didn't appear to be speaking but simply listening, his round apparently calm simple face quite expressionless.

Suddenly Ralph leaned over and said to the psychologist, "What are you in here for?"

The psychologist removed his headphones and said, "It's the ray."

"What ray?"

"It's a ray I see. It's here now."

And all the time he smiled at Ralph with his deceptively rustic face. Of course he would invent a story, but imagine one as crude as a death ray! The psychologist too had a curiously rural accent as if he were a countryman. Of course a good actor could imitate any accent: and one would expect a psychologist to be citified, urbane. That was part of the trickery.

Suddenly he drew away from Ralph and put on his headphones again. A fat nurse was dragging the oxygen apparatus along the floor.

He wanted to phone and tell Linda what had happened, but he had already tried to phone and had got an Emergency Number, whatever that was. It was clear that in the interval of leaving the ward and walking to the phone which was in the corridor someone had made a communication and his call had been redirected. That would happen more and more: in the Mental Home he would probably not be allowed to phone at all. And Linda would not come to visit him.

As he turned round in his bed he saw that the psychologist was gazing at him intently, as if examining him.

And just at that moment also he saw that the hospital was crawling with ministers, like black beetles. They moved from bed to bed peering down at the patients. And then he realized that some of them were priests. One of the latter leaned over his bed and said, "How are you?"

"Fine," he said. The eyes which pretended to be kind were in fact cold. The ministers gathered like vultures round dead bodies. Stocky, applecheeked, they were in fact dangerous enemies: they had been sent for to pass judgement on him, to pronounce him insane.

Then he saw the lawyer striding briskly across to his bed.

"I have made out the will," he said. "You'd better sign it. I'll get two witnesses."

He signed and the lawyer passed the will to one of the ministers, a fat jovial fellow with a red face. The lawyer didn't show the minister the provisions of the will at all, but placed his hand over the document. The minister scrawled his name quickly. So did a youth who was sitting on a chair talking to a patient in the next bed. So that was it: the lawyer didn't really intend to execute the provisions of this will at all. It was all a pretence.

And where was Linda? Now as the final denouement had taken place she would never come again. He closed his eyes. The lawyer disappeared. The ministers and the priests moved like crows among the patients. Another of them leaned over him. He had a squint eye and his hand was fat and flabby. The slant yellow strokes on the cubicle wall dizzied and scarred his eyes. Even if Linda came he would not be able to keep his eyes open. The ministers swarmed about the ward, sucking sustenance from one white shrouded bed after another. They belonged among the dead. They were black bees among white roses. Linda hadn't come, he was finally alone.

In the ambulance the following day there was only himself and the psychologist. He rocked from side to side, and, as he did so, he looked out of the window at the beautiful autumn colours of the day. There were ordinary people walking along the streets with shopping bags in their hands, a boy cycling invulnerably along, a youth and a girl strolling hand in hand. The world that he would never enter again, that he must leave forever behind him. How dear it was, how little he had taken account of its freedom in the past. They left the town and raced along beside a moorland with lochs in it, the untroubled blue of water. How splendid and fine it all was, that heartbreaking picture of serenity. The psychologist smiled at him but didn't speak. Ralph drew his dressing-gown more closely about him as if he were cold. Now and again the ambulance driver waved to a passing van or bus, negligently, cordially.

They had been an hour on the road when they arrived at a large building, along whose side they drove. Eventually they were taken along to a room and told to wait there. Ralph looked up idly and saw that the lamp above the bed had been decorated with a Mexican hat: it was the only odd decoration in the room. This didn't surprise him, it was only another incident in the war of nerves that was being waged against him. Suddenly he saw Linda walking along a corridor and then coming in.

"I raced after you in the car," she said. He was astonished to find her there at all. This appearance didn't seem part of the script he had worked out. According to the scenario he had modelled she should now be sitting with her fat lover drinking wine, being comfortable.

"What did you come here for?" he asked angrily.

"What do you mean what did I come here for? I had to see that you were all right."

"Yes. Now that you have put me here." He wanted to hurt her as badly as he could. He wanted to reduce his dependence on her but he couldn't. He was glad that she had come but he couldn't understand why. This of course was the reason for her visit: she wished to confirm that he had arrived in the Mental Home.

He looked up and saw a grey-haired woman patrolling the corridor. She was going round and round the quadrangle which formed the central core of the hospital. The woman was gaunt, silent, studious: he immediately christened her Lady Macbeth.

"Have you got everything you need?" said Linda anxiously.

"I don't know. I don't care."

"I brought you some money. There might be a shop here." She handed him over some money and he placed it in a locker.

"Do you see that? That hat?" he said aggressively.

She considered it and said, "It's odd right enough. The arm of the lamp looks broken." She switched the lamp on and it emitted a pale light hardly to be seen in the daylight.

"At least it's working," she said.

"Why must it always be something of mine that has something wrong with it?" he asked.

"I don't know. I don't understand. Perhaps it was a nurse's prank."

"Huh."

He was sure it wasn't a nurse's prank. There were too many wrong things, too many coincidences. But what was the inner meaning of leaving a Mexican hat? He was sure it must have some deep inner significance. An allegory, symbolism. But he couldn't work it out.

"You had better go," he said firmly.

"Is that what you want me to do?".

"Yes. That's what I want you to do. You should never have come in the first place."

She regarded him sadly. "I won't be able to come so often now. This place is further away."

"Naturally," he said.

"But I'll do my best."

"I'm sure you will," he said ironically. "How do you get sleep?"

"I don't know," she whispered. Her voice was very low as if there was something wrong with her throat. He was sure that the reason for this was that she was wearing a bug and she wanted only his comments to be picked up.

"I don't want the nurses to hear us quarrelling," she said.

"I don't care," he said. "I know what you're at."

"What do you think I'm at?"

"You have a bug," he whispered. Linda rose to her feet angrily. She was almost weeping but he thought this was her good acting.

"You obviously don't want me here," she said.

"You're right."

But when she did go it was as if his whole life was draining away from him.

Shortly after she had gone a thin tall unsmiling man entered the ward and began to pace from his bed to the opposite wall and then back again. He did this with an obsessive pertinacity, remorselessly, as if he were an automaton. Ralph smiled defensively at him but he didn't smile back. Again he felt fear as if this dour robot might attack him. First there was the grey-haired Lady Macbeth and now this tense unsmiling man from whom emanated an air of suppressed violence.

After a while a man came in with a stethoscope hung over his neck like a snake.

"I'm Doctor Malone," he said in an Irish accent. "If you will wait here for a moment I'll be back for you." Of course he was another spy pretending to be a psychologist. He was handsome, debonair, careless. Suddenly it occurred to Ralph that this was Linda's lover, and not the taxi driver: the whole plot smelt of a psychologist's expertise. And this too was why Linda had come. The plan had been evolved from this very place: he had made a mistake: he hadn't fully realized the complexity of it.

He waited and waited while the thin tense man paced up and down, counting his steps, and when the doctor didn't come he decided that he would go to bed, even though he hadn't been told to. He sat up in bed and watched the relentless repetitive journey of his room mate who completely ignored him. The doctor had left his stethoscope on a neighbouring bed: there was silence everywhere, an oppressive silence. In the middle of it he could hear through the open window the humming of bees. Could he escape from here? Some people had. He couldn't sign himself out, that was certain. He wanted to write something but he couldn't for firstly he couldn't find pen and paper and secondly his concentration had gone.

After a while the doctor came back and said cheerfully, "Come along now if you please."

They sat in chairs opposite each other. The psychologist told him a story as the doctor in the hospital had done and he answered the questions correctly. He was told to remember a certain address which this time was 56 Osborne Street. He analysed it in his mind but couldn't find any connections hanging to it. The psychologist asked him about his novels but he didn't want to talk about them: he knew that Malone hadn't read any of them anyway. The whole place was very quiet: he could hear no violent noises, no mad ravings. The sun shone pleasantly through the windows.

"When will I be out of here?" he asked abruptly.

"Not long," said the psychologist smiling. "Not too long at all." What a Celtic liar you are, thought Ralph. You are like all the Celts, a gentle hypocrite.

"Two weeks?" he probed.

"I wouldn't know about that, not at all," said the psychologist, still smiling. Ralph stared unsmilingly back. In fact he couldn't smile at all nowadays. If he tried to, he felt that his face would crack. He felt like an agent under interrogation: he didn't want to give anything away. Dr Malone took him back to his own room and Ralph pointed to the stethoscope lying on the bed.

"I would forget my own head," said the psychologist.

The thin man was still pacing obsessively up and down. Ralph wanted to ask him about the Mexican hat but decided not to. Suddenly with a brutally quick movement the thin man left the room and Ralph was alone in the overwhelming silence. He waited as if he expected that at any moment a violent madman would burst in, and kill him. The buzzing of the bee was loud in his head which felt as if it would break into pieces. He saw Lady Macbeth on her endless peregrinations. Who would have thought that she had so much blood in her? He stared down at his pyjamas whose stripes matched the stripes of the bee, yellow and black. A breeze stirred the curtains. It occurred to him that they had left him alone like this so that he would attempt to escape but he wasn't going to give them that pleasure.

He stared through the window. Two men with shaven heads and faces as blank and square as loaves were bending down, putting leaves in a wheelbarrow. They gave him a feeling of terrifying desolation. He knew at once that they were patients from the bad wards: they looked inhuman, their movements jerky as in an ancient silent film.

He turned away from the window. The psychologist, whom he had travelled with in the ambulance, was just coming in. He smiled at him and walked over and sat on his bed in the corner. It was all beginning again.

Having a desire to pee he walked along the corridor in search of a bathroom. He found one and went in. There was a man standing there washing his face. Ralph stared into the mirror: his face had become small like a monkey's and his eyes fixed and dull. He thought, So this is what a madman looks like. In the waste of the glass he looked frightened and brutal and vulnerable, all at the same time. He walked slowly back to his room.

The psychologist was sitting on his bed.

"Do you see that ray?" he said.

"No." said Ralph. "I don't see any ray. Where did you see it?"

"It's coming in through the window."

"I don't see anything," said Ralph.

"I have been here before," said the psychologist. "I took aspirins."

"Oh?"

"I was working too hard. I work on a farm."

"Aspirins," said Ralph. "I took sleeping tablets. They found me lying in the middle of a wood. I nearly died," he concluded proudly.

"Aspirins I took," said the psychologist. "I work on a farm," he repeated. "Like hell you do," said Ralph to himself. "Do you think I'm simple?"

"I was here for three weeks," said the psychologist. "They're telling me they're sending me to Glasgow to have a look at my head."

"What treatment is that?" said Ralph.

"I don't know."

"I'd refuse that," said Ralph. "I don't want them to tamper with my brain. If they do that to you, you become like an idiot."

The psychologist didn't answer. It was as if he had used up all his words for the moment.

Ralph felt that he was crossing swords with this psychologist who was pretending to be a farm worker. Why, look at his brow, it was too high for a farm worker's. The psychologist placed all his possessions tidily in his locker. Everything he had was neat and new. His shaving gear was in a black leather case.

Ralph felt like a small boy going to school for the first time. Even now the memory was sharp in his mind. He was wearing short trousers and his knees were bony and pale. There were prefects in uniform all about him. There was a smell of carbolic from the floors and light pouring through the windows as here. The season too was autumn.

The psychologist stared at his ray and then he too went to the bathroom.

That night Ralph sat in the television room along with four or five others, some of whom were sitting silent staring straight ahead of them, some of whom were talking. In the middle of a programme about nurses he suddenly saw three Japanese entering, and speaking in their own language: their faces looked alien and threatening. He knew that this wasn't part of the programme and was about to leave, feeling uneasy and disoriented when a nurse sat beside him and said, "I'm afraid you'll have to change your room tonight if that's all right. I should like to tell you about it. I'll be back later." He turned his face away from the television set and waited for a long time but she didn't come. Later he walked along the corridor to his room. Finding no one there he sat down on his bed. He thought he might phone Linda but decided against it: he was no longer going to be a beggar asking for love. But he felt lonely and dispirited. The fact that the nurse hadn't come to the television room as she had promised bothered him. And he didn't like the idea of changing his room, which was much more comfortable and modern than he had expected. It was true that the patients didn't speak much but they did not look menacing and almost brutal, as the men collecting the autumn leaves had done.

A tall man strode along the corridor carrying a shaving case. He stopped and looked in.

"Hullo," he said. "My name's Heydrich."

"Heydrich?"

"They say that Heydrich is dead but I am Heydrich," the man repeated proudly. "I'll tell you something," he said confidentially. "Hitler was far too lenient with the Jews. If it had been me I would have put them up against a wall and shot the lot of them. That's what they deserved. I told him that but he wouldn't listen." All the time he was talking he looked smiling and pleasant and normal, and Ralph felt the ward spinning about him.

"I keep a Webley at home. I was home for a weekend last weekend. Have you just come? I haven't seen you before."

"That's right," said Ralph. "I came today but they tell me I have to change rooms."

"If I had control here that wouldn't happen," said the tall man. "There are too many Jews about. They're everywhere. Have you met Mr Manson yet? He's a scientist. He's very clever."

"No, I haven't."

"He talks at our meetings, you know. I never say very much. They don't believe I'm Heydrich. They want me to go home but I want to stay here. I've been here before. I was here five years ago, and there was a bulb missing from the bathroom. It's still missing. I don't want to go home. There aren't so many Jews here as you get outside. You'll like Bobby."

"Bobby?"

"He's the male nurse. He's the one who keeps our razors."

Ralph stared at him.

"Didn't you know. They take your razor from you and they keep it in the office. When you want a shave in the morning you have to collect it."

"Should I hand it in just now then?"

"You can leave it for a while. I'm going to have a shower. I like to keep clean. That was one of the troubles with the Jews. They never washed, they smelt. In the Reich cleanliness was very important. I can't stand dirt."

Suddenly Ralph said, "Do you know anything about a Mexican hat?"

"Mexican hat?"

"Yes, if you look up there you'll see a Mexican hat. And there's something wrong with the arm of the lamp. It's been twisted."

"I don't know about that. There might have been a fancy dress party. I don't like that myself. I prefer efficiency. Take yesterday now. The food in the canteen was rotten. I told the supervisor that she should put the staff up against the wall and shoot them. She reported me. It's very important to be efficient. That's how the Reich became so great. Sometimes in the office they can't find your razor right away or they put the wrong name on it. I gave them a row about that. But they are quite nice usually and I didn't notice any Jews among them. I like it here. I don't want to go home. I've been here five months. The other time it was four months."

"Can you get newspapers here?"

"I don't get one. I used to get the *Record* but I stopped it. I'm not sure if they bring newspapers now. Some of us are allowed down town you know. You could ask someone to bring you one back from the shop."

"When will we be allowed down town?"

"It might be a week or two. Or more. I go to the canteen but I don't often go down town."

"Canteen?"

"There's a canteen. You can buy cigarettes and sweets there. I'll show you where it is if you like."

At that moment Ralph saw a procession of men walking along the corridor, each carrying a cup of coffee or tea. He didn't want to mention it to the tall man in case he was imagining it. The men were holding the cups steady, staring ahead as if they were part of a moving frieze.

Heydrich? How could anyone be Heydrich? On the other hand the man might have been sent to further disorientate him. He was sure that Linda was now the Irish psychologist's lover and that they were staying together in a flat in this very town. If he phoned her she would not be at home.

"Can you phone from here?" he asked the tall man.

"There's a phone in the corridor. It's outside the television room."

"I think I'll walk along then."

"See you," said the tall man waving his white towel. He must have decided that I'm not a Jew, thought Ralph.

When Ralph phoned it was a long time before anyone answered. Finally he recognized the voice of his mother-in-law.

"Where's Linda?" he asked.

"She's in bed." His mother-in-law sounded hostile.

"I don't believe it. I don't believe she's there at all."

"She's tired. She's in bed." He slammed the phone down and walked back along the corridor. Of course she wasn't in bed. She had organized this with the Irish psychologist from the very beginning. He remembered her saying once, "I've always wanted to be a nurse." Maybe she had meant that she wanted to work in a hospital like this. "They do a useful job. Their work is more important than yours."

"I give pleasure to people," he had said defensively.

"Well, maybe, but you're an élitist. You prefer books to people deep down."

"That's right," he had said. "Their conversation is more interesting."

He had never understood 'ordinary' people. For instance they were very conscious of precedence: no one was more reactionary than an 'ordinary' person. Once on a train travelling to Edinburgh he had met a drunk who had said to him, "I don't like you. You think I'm not good enough for you. But I'll tell you something, I'm better than you." The drunk had thrust his face at him like a damp torch and he had finally retreated to another compartment. Ordinary people were like another race: they read the *Sun* and the *Star*.

But he was sure that Linda had turned against him, against his egotism, his élitism. The Irish psychologist hadn't looked at all élitist but rather cheerful and relaxed. He couldn't bear the thought that Linda should be with him. Nor could he bear the thought that he would never be able to read again.

Through the window he could see birds flying about in the twilight. On the lawn there was an exotic tree with pink blossoms, but he couldn't identify it. It had a thick trunk and the blossoms flamed like candles. He didn't know much about trees or birds: all he knew about was words. Of course Linda was not in bed and that business about tiredness was an excuse. The light faded from the sky: he thought he could hear the distant sound of the television set.

A handicapped girl who walked to one side like a ship in a

storm ran pale-faced to him and said, "Are you Mr Simmons?"

"Yes."

"There's a phone call for you."

He knew it was from Linda but he didn't want to answer it. His mother-in-law would have phoned the Irish psychologist's flat and Linda would now be phoning from there. He was determined that he wouldn't phone her but in spite of his decision he found himself walking quickly along the corridor with the reproductions of Picasso and Klee on the walls. He picked up the phone. Her voice sounded far away and gentle.

"I just got up," she said. She sounded punch drunk. But then she was a good actress.

"Where are you phoning from?" he asked.

"Where do you think I'm phoning from?"

"All right. Put the phone down and I'll dial your number," he said.

"If you want." And he did what he had said. The phone rang and she answered it. But he was sure that engineers had been hired to construct this piece of trickery: he wasn't speaking to the house at all. Linda's voice sounded far too remote and wavering. She began to weep at the other end of the phone. Satisfied, he put the phone down slowly.

That night he was shifted into another room where there was a full complement of patients, that is, four including himself. Nurses came in with a trolley and doled out tablets: and in the morning they were wakened at half-past six. He had to go along to the office to collect his razor, and he shaved with the others silently in the bathroom. When he returned to his room two young nurses were trying to waken the young boy in the adjacent bed.

"Come on now, Ronny," they pleaded with him. But he crouched under the bedclothes and wouldn't obey them.

"Now, Ronny," said one of the sisters who came in at this point as if she was doing it quite often, "you must get out of your bed like the rest. Otherwise you know what will happen." But he turned away from her, burying his head in the pillow. After a while the sister went out.

In the opposite bed to Ralph was a squat man of about sixty or so who had a white moustache like a ghostly officer from the First World War: he made up his bed very meticulously, a towel still draped about his neck. Ralph made up his own bed though he wasn't very satisfied with it; however he left it as it was.

"Look, I'll show you how you to it," said the man who introduced himself as Hugh, Hugh Green. "You didn't tuck it in at the bottom, you see." He padded about in his bedroom slippers.

The youth turned and tossed restlessly in his bed. The psychologist, who had been shifted into this room as well, replaced the shaving articles in his leather case. Ralph was reminded again of his days in boarding school.

"Did you sleep well?" said Hugh Green.

"Yes."

"I sleep till four o'clock in the morning. After that I don't sleep at all." Hugh went and pulled the bedclothes away from the youth.

"This is Ronny," he said. "He never gets up in the morning. And he's very noisy when he is up, aren't you, Ronny? He won't take his tablets," said Hugh. Ralph glanced across to Ronny's locker. On it there was a bottle of orangeade and a record called 'Breakdown'. The title of the record worried him as if it had been placed there like a theatrical prop to remind him of his illness. Hugh took out a cigarette and began to smoke. Restlessly he went out into the corridor and came back again. He slid his feet along as if he were on wheels.

"Have you been here before?" said Ralph to him.

"Yes, I took aspirins. I was here for three weeks about five years ago."

It occurred to Ralph that all the people he had met had tried to commit suicide by means of an overdose: he wondered if the youth had done the same. Surely this wasn't a coincidence. On the contrary everything was a reminder of his own attempted suicide. He sat on his bed staring dully at the floor. Hugh padded out into the corridor again smoking furiously. The psychologist took a bag of sweets from his locker and offered them but Ralph didn't take any. Suddenly the sister came in again in a rush of white and blue.

"Now, listen," she said to Ronny. "You have to get up." And she pulled the bedclothes to the floor leaving him cowering against his sheets in his striped pyjamas. Ronny rubbed his eyes and stared around him.

"You shouldn't be watching the tv till all hours," she said. Ronny got up and made his way to the bathroom.

"That boy," she said, shaking her head and going out again.

All this appeared to Ralph like a scene from a play. Around him were four actors. What organization it all required, what attention to detail.

"Listen," he said to Hugh. "I can't read. Are you like that?"

"Yes. I tried to read but I can't. My wife brought me a lot of history books. I should be making notes on them but I can't do it." He put out his cigarette and lit another, offering Ralph one from his packet. Ralph took it.

"As a matter of fact," said Hugh, "you weren't supposed to take that cigarette. You're not supposed to lend or borrow money either. Did you not read the rules?"

"No," said Ralph. He picked up the sheet with the rules: there were a number of misspellings and errors in punctuation. This too bothered him quite a lot. He was sure that they were fake, hastily put together for his benefit. He wondered whether Hugh had deliberately made him break the rules. He stubbed his cigarette in a blue scarred ashtray.

Ronny came back from the bathroom, tall and strutting. Ralph saw that his face was pale and spotty. It was really astonishing how an actor as young as this could be hired.

"I hope you washed yourself," said Hugh. "You needed a wash." He walked over to Ronny on his slippered feet.

"Listen to him," said Ronny in a high almost hysterical voice. "He never washes himself. Do you, old man? You never wash do you, old man?" Hugh turned away, the cigarette between his lips, smiling.

"He just washes his moustache," said Ronny in the same high voice, and went off into a paroxysm of laughter. "He takes it off at night and leaves it beside his bed, don't you, old man?" He seemed very noisy and aggressive. Hugh smiled patiently and then went out of the room and along the corridor. He seemed constitutionally unable to sit still.

"Old man," Ronny shouted after him. He made up his bed quickly and noisily drank some orangeade. Hugh came back and went over to him and punched him lightly in the chest.

"You know what's going to happen to you," he said. "You'll end up in another ward, one of the really bad ones, if you don't

140

take your pills and if you don't get up in time in the morning. And if you don't wash."

"Listen to him. He snores," said Ronny and went off into another paroxysm of laughter. "Did you hear him snoring? He snores like a horse. You're a horse, old man, a horse, a horse."

"That's right, I'm a horse," said Hugh calmly. He put out his cigarette and lit another one. "You've taken my ashtray," he said to Ronny. "You don't smoke and you take my ashtray all the time. You're a thief, aren't you? Aren't you?"

"I'm a thief, I'm a thief, I'm a thief," Ronny chanted.

What actors they are, thought Ralph. They have rehearsed this very carefully. What looks spontaneous is really planned and scripted. They're really very good.

Hugh walked over to Ronny again and said, "I'm serious. If you don't watch out you'll end up in another ward."

"I don't care," said Ronny. "I've been in one before. I don't mind. There's more action there. There's no action here, is there, old man?"

"Action?"

"And I'll tell you another thing. These pills you're taking make you impotent. That's why your wife doesn't visit you. His wife never comes to see him," he said to Ralph. "'Cos he's impotent and he smells. Don't you, old man?" Hugh smiled tolerantly. "It's true though she never comes to see you. And you smoke too much. You'll die of smoking, old man."

"Ronny watched the television till midnight," said Hugh. "What was it last night, Ronny? Was it *Frankenstein*? Ronny here never got his O levels, did you, Ronny? He wasn't in school long enough. You were jinking, weren't you, Ronny? You wait till that sister comes. She's got it in for you."

"I did," chanted Ronny. "I did get my O levels. You don't even know what O levels are. They weren't invented when you were in school, old man." And he doubled up with laughter.

"Run away and polish your head," said Hugh calmly.

"Polish your head, polish your head," Ronny chanted, laughing again with a high nervous noisy sound. Everything he did was tense and nervous and jerky as if he were a twanging wire, while all the time the psychologist smiled in the corner, now and again getting up to tidy his bed compulsively.

"Breakfast," said Hugh, glancing at his watch.

"What kind of watch is that?" said Ronny. "That's a Russian watch. The old man is a Communist. What Communist gave you that watch, old man?"

"I'm going for my breakfast," said Hugh and padded out of the room. After a while, Ralph and the psychologist followed him.

"I don't want any breakfast," shouted Ronny. Ralph and the psychologist walked along side by side past the office. Ralph wanted to speak to his companion: his silence bothered him. He hated being judged by that silence; and yet when he was writing there was nothing he liked better. He hadn't talked much to Linda thinking that in comparison with his own, her concerns were trivial. He would have liked to have been self-sufficient as a stone. Yet here he wished to speak.

"I wonder what they'll have for breakfast," he said.

"I don't know," said the psychologist, but didn't add to his statement. What a clever fellow he is, thought Ralph, he is doing this deliberately. And he was ashamed of himself for having spoken first as if it had been a culpable weakness.

They queued for their food and then sat at the same table. By now Ralph could recognize one or two people, including Lady Macbeth and the tall thin man whom he had seen pacing up and down in the ward the day before, and who had clearly been shifted. People stared morosely down at their plates. Opposite him sat an old man whose mouth moved continually, as if he were in the process of having a stroke. Now and again he would find someone staring at him and then he would remind himself that after all this was a drama group which had been hired to drive him mad.

"You must take your food," said a nurse to a young girl who was standing at the door.

"I don't want to."

"You must take it. The doctor said you had to take it." The young girl sat sulkily at a table near the door but made no attempt to eat.

When they had finished their food the handicapped girl, who had told him about the phone call, cleaned all the tables and cleared the plates away. She looked white-faced and angry, as if the diners offended her by their slovenly manners. After breakfast was over, Ralph followed the others into the lounge.

When he had had his pills in the lounge carefully dispensed from a trolley, he walked back to his room. Ronny was sitting on his bed staring down at the floor.

"Should you not be taking some pills?" said Ralph.

"I'm not taking them."

After a while he added, "I'll get the bastard yet."

"What bastard?"

"My stepfather."

"Your stepfather?"

"That's right. He's a naval officer."

Stepfather, thought Ralph. So they're at it again. And a picture of his own stepfather returned to him, silent and bookish, always disapproving. Perhaps that was why he himself had become a novelist, creating new worlds for himself to escape that terrible silence. If only his stepfather had once shouted at him but, no, whenever he did anything wrong or was too noisy, then that awful silence had descended: he had felt himself less important than one of his stepfather's books. What was the secret of those books, their calming cold secret mystery? He must try and find out. And so he had tried to read them, to placate his stepfather, as if by reading he might enter that world and, little by little, he had done so. Had he done the same with Linda, repeated the silences which he himself had endured? Had he cast his disapproval on her too? But, no, that did not excuse her, unless she had grown to hate him as much as he himself had hated his stepfather. And now he in turn had entered the kingdom of silence. It was his weapon as it had been his stepfather's. The sins of the stepfathers are visited on the children.

"He beat me up, the bastard," said Ronny. "But he won't do it again. I'm bigger than him now."

"What did he beat you for?" said Ralph.

"For nothing. He took it into his head. Because of school sports. Report cards. Anything."

"And what about your mother?"

Ronny snorted but didn't answer. Ralph thought of the mother as suave, svelte, ambitious, dressed in fine clothes, standing beside her husband at parties. He said, "You should take your pills, you know, or they'll put you in a worse ward."

"I don't care. I've been in one already. I like the nut cases."

143

"As if you are not one yourself," thought Ralph. But the cunning of the scheme almost overwhelmed him. Imagine putting him in with a stepson, just as he had been himself. Was there nothing that they hadn't thought of? The labyrinthine plot attracted him, repelled him. It was so huge, so luminous in its ramifications. It was almost beyond the scope of the human mind. How much he had underestimated Linda. It was she who was the novelist, not him.

"So one day I left the house and I swallowed a lot of aspirins," Ronny was saying. "I couldn't stand the bastard any longer."

"I tried everything," Ralph thought, "I abased myself. I read his books even though I didn't understand them. I wanted to know his secret, to enter his world, to make him notice me. But he didn't notice me. There was nothing I could do that would make him notice me. There was only that terrible silence as cold as crystal. It was as if he hated me for existing, for being an interruption to his books."

His head spun: he couldn't understand what was happening to him. It was as if, even while he was growing up, this plot was being woven about him: everything that had happened to him, everything that he was, contributed to this story which was torturing him.

And a kind of tenderness for Ronny overwhelmed him. "Please," he said. "Please. Take your pills."

Ronny raised his head as if the tone of Ralph's voice had attracted him: he hearkened like a dog that is listening to a sound that no human ear can hear.

"I might," he said. "I might at that."

And suddenly Ralph began to tell him his own story. He told him of the hotel, of the black doctor, of the tapes, the taxi driver, he told him of his journey into the wood, and Ronny listened seriously.

But he did not really appear interested till Ralph told him about his own stepfather, of his silences, of his disapproval. Nevertheless while he was talking to him Ralph was thinking, This boy is an actor, he has been planted here. There can be no other explanation, there have been too many coincidences. Why should I be confiding in an actor, whose profession is being used to destroy me. Yet some impulse had made him break his silence, speak endlessly as if he were talking to himself.

144

"I'll tell you something, he makes me feel like shit," said Ronny. "I'll strangle the bastard." And his face became ugly and angry so that Ralph felt frightened that the boy might attack him. And then it occurred to him, That is what they are gambling on, that this boy might confuse me with his stepfather, that in the middle of the night he might attack me with a banned razor. And he was frightened again and wanted to leave the ward, but he stayed. Sometimes now he didn't care whether he was killed or not. It might not last very long anyway, the fact of death, it might last only a moment, the stab in the stomach, the strangling, the throttling. And in any case what did he have to look forward to? This boy would be doing him a favour.

Should he not simply say to him, "I am your stepfather," and let events take their course? Should he not tender himself as a sacrifice to that desperate rage?

He remembered the night he had shouted at his stepfather, "I'll burn the house down. Send for the police. I don't care." And his father standing by the phone saying, "I will. Don't think I won't."

And himself, "Do it then." And at that moment if he had had a match he would have burnt the house down. His stepfather trembled and shook, his face was twisted with hatred and helplessness, and his mother had come between them and said, "If you send for the police you'll ruin his life, don't you understand?" And he hated his mother then and always. How had she married this iceberg? Could she not see what he was like? That he had no love in his bones? And sometimes in the night he had heard them whispering together and thought that they were talking about him.

Ronny was looking at him with a hostile gaze now. He was saying, "I've changed my mind. I won't take the pills. They can do what they like." And he stalked out of the ward with the careless stride of youth that does not think of consequences. And Ralph was left alone again.

He walked to the window. The leaves were stirring in a breeze and the two men were gathering them in their wheelbarrow. It was to a ward such as they inhabited that Ronny might be sent if he continued with his disobedience. Ralph glanced up at the hat which hung above the lamp but realized that this was not the ward it was in.

145

He took a pad from his locker and tried to write but he could write nothing. Then very seriously in the silence of the room he began to note down reasons why he believed there was a plot against him. He headed his notes THE PLOT and numbered his reasons as if he were a bureaucrat.

1. Why did the lawyer say, "This is like a scene from a play"?
2. Why did the trolleys in the previous hospital have only two wheels instead of four?
3. Why was there a Mexican hat on the light?
4. Why have I been put in here with a boy who has a stepfather?
5. Why did the surgeon drop the match on my pillow?
6. Why is the psychologist always watching me?
7. Why did that nurse say, "I could make a scene if I liked"?
8. Why did Linda pretend that she was tired? Why didn't she answer the phone?
9. Why is it that everyone I meet has taken an overdose?
10. How could a black doctor be called Emmanuel?

He studied what he had written and tried to think of other items to record but he seemed for the moment to have exhausted his questions. He would present his list to that lady psychologist when he had his first meeting with her. He would show her that he was not to be trifled with, that he had a clear cool brain, that he had read psychology and knew what he was talking about.

Finally he thought of another question, Why was there a procession of men carrying coffee cups in the corridor?

"Oh, that," said Hugh. "There's a coffee machine along there. Do you want to come along for a coffee?"

Ralph and Hugh and the psychologist walked along the corridor together, Hugh scuttling along very fast as was usual with him. They passed Lady Macbeth who was pacing up and down in her endless circles. A woman in a nightgown came out of a room and said, "Why is my room full of tourists? They came on a bus and they are lying in the beds. Where did they come from? You tell me that."

"Tourists?" said Hugh.

146

"Tourists. I can't understand their language. They came off the bus and into my room. Why did they choose my room? They didn't come for Bed and Breakfast, I can tell you." She thrust her haunted face towards them. "I've had Americans and I should know. There was a woman came to my house one day and she examined the sheets, and she said, 'I think they will do'. 'Well,' I said to her, and I grabbed her skirt and looked at her underskirt and I said to her, 'Do you think that is clean enough for my sheets?' She didn't like it."

"You'll be all right," said Hugh. "They're not tourists. What nationality do you think they are?"

"I think they're Germans."

"They're not Germans anyway," said Hugh. "I was in the war."

"Well then they might be Dutch. They're not so bad. I had a Dutch boy in my house and he took pictures all the time. Even when I was at the sink he was taking pictures. But then he began to steal my things. He stole my ornaments and then he stole my dog."

"They're all right if they're Dutch," said Hugh.

And the three of them walked along to the coffee machine.

"There was no one there," said Hugh. "No one at all."

When they got back to their room Hugh lit another cigarette. "I don't know if my wife will come today. I gave my sons my business, you know, after I came out of the hospital last time."

The other two waited for him to continue.

"I have two sons and I divided the business between them. I wanted to get on with my writing."

"Writing?" said Ralph.

"I'm writing a history of the world from a Communist point of view. I make notes all the time. I have a typewriter but I know a professional typist who will put a finish on the book for me."

"How long will it take?" said Ralph.

"I don't know yet. It'll take a long time. It hasn't been done before. Wells wrote a history of the world but it wasn't from a Communist point of view. I'm a Communist. My sons aren't Communist though. I have a paper business."

"Where is it?"

"In Bowling." He paused and then said, "Who built the pyramids? I ask you that. It was the ordinary people. It's always the rich who are written about, the kings and so on. But it's the poor who did the work. I've got hundreds of cards on which I've written

147

notes. My wife threw some of them out; she said she couldn't move in her own house. She might come today, I don't know. My sons are too busy to come."

"Why did you start on a book like that?" said Ralph.

"I don't know. Yet I had plenty of other hobbies. I used to bowl but I stopped that. And I used to be a curler. But that wasn't enough. I wanted to find out what history was all about. I left school at the age of fifteen but I always had an inquiring mind." He stubbed out his cigarette and lit another one, padding restlessly about the room, oldish, restless with a grey moustache.

"I write books," Ralph volunteered suddenly.

"You mean you publish them?"

"That's right."

"You could maybe tell me what you have to do, then, to get a book published. I'll try and publish it when I'm finished."

"You must have it neatly typed," said Ralph, "and then you send it away to a publisher. Some publishers specialize in certain subjects. I don't know who would publish your book. It's a big thing, isn't it?"

"It is. I don't know when I'll finish it. I wanted my wife to bring me some books last time but she forgot. I wanted to take notes but I can't seem to concentrate. I used to be able to concentrate. I used to work till four in the morning. But I can't concentrate here. I think it must be the drugs."

The psychologist was listening carefully but not speaking. "What's it like when you leave the hospital?" he asked eventually.

"What do you mean?"

"When you come out. What's it like? What do people think?"

"Nothing. They don't think anything of it nowadays," said Hugh expansively. "In the old days they did but not now. They think of it now as an illness. It didn't bother me. People used to come up and speak to me just the same. I started on my book again when I left the hospital. I worked very hard at it. And then I got another depression and tried to kill myself again. The house is full of these cards. My wife is always complaining. I'm working on the history of the Trade Unions just now. There's a lot in that."

"I'm sure," said Ralph. "But the main thing is to have it typed neatly." He couldn't imagine the appalling labour this man was involved in: it made him tired just to think about it. Why, he couldn't even read a column of the *Daily Express* himself.

"What paper do you read?" he asked.

"I read the *Sun* and the *Star*. At one time I used to read the *Telegraph* but it gives you a wrong slant on things: it's very Tory. I used to read the *Financial Times* as well."

So here was another actor who pretended to have delusions about authorship. First of all there was a stepson and then a potential author. What an extraordinary thing: the coincidences were bizarre and therefore not coincidences at all. And all the time the psychologist was silent: he had an infinite capacity for vigilance.

Hugh stopped talking and sat on his bed smoking. Then he walked out into the corridor again. Time passed so slowly, there was no end to it. He must ask that Irish psychologist again how long he was likely to be in. He might be here forever. And Hugh's wife would never come to see him, that was certain. She too had betrayed her husband, she would have mixed up all his cards while he was in hospital and when he arrived home there would be such a chaos that he would go mad again. And again, why had he been so silly as to hand over his business to his sons? Would men never learn the infinite greed of the human heart?

When the lady psychologist sent for him he took his list of complaints with him. She was sitting at a desk, a charge nurse beside her. Did she need a witness in case he attacked her?

"How are you feeling today?" she asked brightly. "Do you still think you're being spied on?" Wordlessly he handed her the list and she glanced rapidly over it.

"What is this?" she said.

"Proof," he answered tersely.

"Proof of what?"

"That I'm being spied on. That it's all a charade." The charge nurse didn't smile nor make any sign at all. He simply listened.

"What is this about a Mexican hat?" she asked the charge nurse.

"I don't know. I'll look into it."

"On the light," she said to Ralph. "It must be a mistake. Nothing important. Someone playing a prank."

"To you nothing is important," said Ralph. "That's where you're wrong. Everything is important. Everything is linked. You think I'm ignorant. I'm not. I've read Freud and Jung. I know more than you think."

"And what is this about a surgeon dropping a match on a pillow? I don't understand any of this."

"It was in the other hospital," said Ralph. "He obviously wanted to get me into trouble."

"And what's this about a stepson? Do you know anything about this?" she asked the charge nurse.

"There's a patient called Ronny in the same room. He's a stepson."

"Oh, I see," and she smiled for the first time. "And because you're a stepson you think that we. . . . Jolly funny."

"Not at all funny," said Ralph indignantly. "More tragic than funny if you ask me." He wanted to shout at this woman who didn't seem to be listening to anything he was saying.

"Tell me about your wife," said the psychologist briskly.

"What about her?"

"Have you been making any bad phone calls to her?" Bad, as if he was a child.

"No."

"But you must believe that she loves you. She is coming to see you tomorrow. She phoned to tell me."

"I don't want her to come. I want her to stay away. When will I be out of here?"

"Oh, it won't be too long if you behave yourself. But you do believe that she loves you, that she worries about you."

"Love," he said, "what does that mean? The world is so meagre. I saw that in Yugoslavia."

"Meagre?" she said. He felt that he had already mentioned this to her but he couldn't remember. The desk in front of her was bare, meagre. That was how the world was. Flat, without depth. The bareness, the lack of ornament, the invincible presence of things, their demand to be heard.

The charge nurse was looking at him intently, and fiddling with a pencil.

"I don't understand what you mean by love," said Ralph. "How do we know?"

"How do we know what?"

"What people are thinking. They may be talking to you about one thing and thinking of something else. How can we see inside their heads? We have our own theatres inside our heads."

150

"I see." She glanced at the charge nurse. "But you haven't been making threatening phone calls."

"No."

"I'm sorry about that stepson, that Ronny. I didn't realize. . . . You didn't like your stepfather, did you?"

"No."

"He lived in a world of his own, didn't he? He was always reading."

"Where did you get that from? Has Linda been talking to you?"

"No. You told me yourself." The woman's glasses glinted in the sparse autumnal sunshine which shone through the window behind her.

"Did I?" said Ralph. "I can't remember. But it's true. He did live in a world of his own. I tried to get into it but I couldn't."

"And it wasn't a meagre world, was it?"

"No. Eventually I got into it. But when I was a child it was hard."

"You mean as a child you never got into that world."

"No, I didn't. I wondered about it. How he could be so self-sufficient. How he didn't need me. How he didn't seem to know my name. Sometimes when I spoke to him it was as if he was coming out of a trance. He had a large bald head."

"What?"

"A large bald head. I used to watch. It was like a big marble with veins in it. And his eyes were always cold. As if he was saying to me that I had no right to exist. I used to wonder if he ever thought about me at all."

"Did you think he was plotting against you?"

"I used to hear my mother and him whispering in their bed at night. I used to listen at the keyhole but I could never make out the words."

"As in Yugoslavia?"

"What do you mean?"

"People talked around you there and you didn't know what they were saying. Isn't that right?"

For the first time he regarded her with a wary respect.

"That's true," he said slowly. "I didn't think of that."

"You have a high opinion of yourself, don't you? You believe that no one can understand things except yourself. You

151

under-estimate other people just as your stepfather did. You never listen to them. When did you listen to anyone last?"

"I listen to the characters in my books."

"That's different. When did you listen to any living people? You despise me: you are surprised that I should have any interesting thoughts. You think you know more than I do about my own subject. And yet what I have said is quite obvious. In Yugoslavia you couldn't make out what people were saying any more than you could make out what your father and mother were saying in bed at night. What happened to you in Yugoslavia?"

"Nothing much. We visited a cave."

"A cave?" The word hung hollowly between them.

"Yes," he said, "an icy cave. It was so cold."

"An icy cave?" She echoed him.

"Yes," he said. "It was so cold. In the bowels of the earth." After he had said the word "bowels" he wondered why he had used it. It sounded like a cliché.

"And all around," he said, "there were faces and bodies, all of ice."

"Did any of them remind you of your father?"

"He used to play chess. He never played against people. He played out problems from the *Observer* and the *Sunday Times*. There was a chess player among the figures."

"In the cave?"

"Yes."

"Anything else? Did you visit anywhere else?"

"We visited a sort of colosseum. There was no roof on it." He stopped again, thinking.

"A building without a roof?"

"Yes."

"Why wasn't it finished?"

"Because the fairies who had been building it flew away at dawn."

"Jolly good." The woman pushed papers about on her desk and said, "Now don't you be rude or violent to your wife when she visits you. She is suffering a great deal and she loves you, whether you believe it or not. Otherwise she wouldn't come at all. She phones me up to find out how you are."

"She would wouldn't she?"

"What do you mean?"

"She wants to know how her play is progressing. In any case this place is a theatre not a real hospital."

"Did your father take notes?" she asked him obliquely glancing down at the list he had brought her.

"When?"

"For instance, when he was reading a book?"

"Yes, he did. He left hundreds of notes in jotters when he died."

"What did you do with them?"

"I kept them. I sometimes use them in my novels."

"What were they about?"

"Oh, about lots of things. Comments on life. Notes on books he had read."

There was another silence and then she said, "Well, I think you're making progress. I'll see you again shortly. Meanwhile you can go along to your room."

"There is one other thing," he said. "About King Lear."

"What about King Lear?"

"A man in my ward says that he gave his business away to his children. They never come to see him."

"Who is this gentleman?" said the psychologist to the charge nurse.

"I think he must be talking about Hugh. He comes from Bowling. He says that he gave away his business to his sons."

"I know you're an actor as well," said Ralph to the charge nurse, and for a moment there was a flicker of what might have been malice in the latter's eyes.

"Cut along now," said the psychologist. "I'll see you soon. But you are feeling better?"

"Yes. A little."

"Jolly good."

There was a flash of hockey sticks in his mind, girls in green uniforms, a green field with an umpire in it. And then he was out of the room.

"Excuse me," he said to Lady Macbeth who was passing in her ashen helmet. It was as if she was sleepwalking, having surrendered a precious kingdom as well.

He got it into his head that he didn't have the courage of Ronny. Why, if he was a real writer at all, he should enter the other wards, the mad ones, the lower circles, he should listen to the mad songs, the elegies, but he was afraid. But surely before he left here he must enter these wards, he must find out what it was like to be at the extreme limits of existence. In the place without music, without harmony. He must talk to these two flat-faced crew-cut lunatics who walked about slowly, perpetually shovelling the autumn leaves into their barrows, gathering wounded nature from the world of wind and rain. He had not faced life: and this was what had happened to him. He had not looked into the darkest corners with his torch. He admired Ronny, large, noisy, careless.

"I don't care," said Ronny. "I'll go there but I won't take my pills." It seemed to him that Ronny symbolized all those men of free spirit by which the human race had been impelled up the shaky ladder of evolution from the rank green nameless grass.

"The old men are funny," said Ronny. "I like them."

When Linda came to visit him he told her about this. She looked at him with large dry eyes as if she were stunned.

"What are you talking about?"

"I know what I'm talking about. I haven't suffered enough yet. You started me on the road but I must go further along it."

"I started you on it?"

"Yes. With your drama. I wish you would come out into the open."

She was wearing her red velvet suit and looked neat and desirable. He regarded her with hopeless longing. She had brought sweets and oranges. He showed her the first verse of a poem he had written.

> And as we wave goodbye
> I know we shall not meet again
> either here or earnestly
> in another place beyond this pain.

He saw the tears springing to her eyes. Oh, how clever she was, what duplicity she had.

"You must know an engineer as well," he said. "He has done something to the phone."

Through the window he could see Heydrich and the handicapped girl strolling among the autumn leaves hand in hand. Heydrich tall and blonde talking to her in an animated manner.

"What kind of tree is that?" he asked Linda, pointing out to the lawn. The tree leaned like a cherry tree towards the ground with its umbrella of pink petals.

"I don't know. I haven't seen one like that before." Heydrich and the girl passed under the splendid heart-breaking tree.

"The man there thinks he is Heydrich," he said.

"Oh?"

"Apart from that he's okay. Of course he's an actor. He's trained for the part. I must say he's very good."

For a moment there, there was a gap and he saw through it, and the gap closed again,

"The psychologist says you may not be long in here. Maybe another two weeks."

"I know I'll be here a long time," said Ralph. "I know I'll be here forever."

"Why do you say that?"

"The logic of the plot demands it."

"What plot?"

"The plot has an invincible rightness. I've been caught in my own plot. My stepfather saw to that. And there's a boy here exactly like me. And a man who gave away his property just like King Lear. He's trying to be a writer too. And his wife mixes up his notes. There are too many things. . . ." He rubbed his head. "The comprehensive power of the plot. Sometimes I feel as if I'm inside a machine."

"You know I love you," said Linda tearfully. "You know there is no one else but you. You know that, don't you?" Her voice echoed mockingly as if from the inside of a cave.

"So you say."

"But it's true. I've always loved you."

"Why should you love me? I can't see why you should. There's no reason for it."

"Of course there's no reason for it. That's what you don't understand. That is what love is."

"Love!"

"It's caring for someone. Surely you can see that. I care for you. I don't want to see you like this." And she cried again, trembling and shaking. But he regarded her with a cold eye. Who could believe anything that anyone said. In the last analysis everyone was out for himself. All the ethical systems that had ever been woven like a spurious tapestry were a lot of crap: tiny men with tiny teeth had nibbled and nibbled till they had climbed the ladder from which they could see whole landscapes. The world was an eternal spy story with double agents, triple agents, secret scripts. A man must always look over his shoulder to check if he was being followed. Even the most innocent spectator, that one lounging by the lamp-post, was part of the plot.

"If you could only come straight out with it," he said. "Admit it."

"Admit what?"

"That you've found someone else. It would be much simpler. That psychologist. You've said you always wanted to be a nurse. That you never liked being a secretary. That you didn't think it was useful."

"But . . . what psychologist? Who are you talking about?"

"The Irish one. The one who came to see me first. I suppose you could call him handsome. Perhaps even charming. He's certainly handsomer than the taxi driver. And something as complicated as this would require a psychologist. Then again your mother was a nurse. Perhaps there's a secret union which looks after its own. Look, how do we know what happens in hospitals? They've got the power of life and death over their patients. They can kill them, sign certificates. Hospitals are secret closed societies. The word goes out. This fellow is making a nuisance of himself. Let's get rid of him."

She stared at him in astonishment as if the fertility of his imagination had stunned her. In her infernal reds, in which fires were burning, he saw the glow of the tree behind her. Petals lay on the ground below it. Everything was burning away, but was it being resurrected?

He saw a police car swing up the drive and draw up at the door of the bad wards.

A nurse swirling a red and navy-blue cloak passed like a foreign exotic bird along the pathway.

"Maybe you can't help what you're doing," he said. "Maybe none of us can."

"I shan't be able to come tomorrow," Linda said tiredly. "I'll come the day after that. It's a long drive and mother isn't well."

"I'm sure she isn't."

"She isn't. She doesn't know what is happening. She doesn't understand."

"But I do," said Ralph proudly. "I understand."

"My mother likes you."

"No, she doesn't. She doesn't understand what I do. She wishes you had married someone else. She has the old-fashioned idea that writing isn't work, not like nursing. It's not respectable."

"Well, you've got to make allowances for that."

"Why should I be making allowances all the time?"

"I don't know. I make allowances too," said Linda. "We all have to make allowances. That among other things is what marriage is."

Like Dante I must enter the final circle, he thought. I must burn there and find out about the fire and the mad shadows. That is what the Inferno is, the seethe of lost egos burning in their pain.

"Do you remember Mrs Hunter?" said Linda briskly. "She phoned Annie Macleod and asked her who had hired Judas to betray Christ. Would you believe that?"

"And who did?"

"What?"

"Who did hire him? She has a point there. She's no fool."

Linda ignored this comment and proceeded. "And Mary Mason has a black baby. Her husband is a black doctor in Liverpool, I think it is."

Ralph thought of the house surrounded by its gravel. It seemed to him that the ferns and grasses were rising up to swallow him. Once he had been hacking at ferns when his glasses, which he kept in his top jacket pocket, fell into the greenery. Blindly he had searched for them but couldn't find them. Such a failed scholar among famished nature he was. There was some deep meaning in the incident. Nature which he had seen by means of his glasses now became a blur as he thrust his arms into the luxuriant greenery, which had closed over them. Sometimes he had felt the vegetation was devouring even his manuscripts, turning them first green and then brown. And on rainy days he watched the water pour into the brimming barrel which stood under the rone. Another day he had seen two rabbits playing in the garden. No, he said to them, this is not an Irish missal, the real weasel is waiting for you. Even now he is feeling his way towards you, he is preparing his dance of luminous rings.

157

"Is there anything you want me to bring you?" said Linda.

"No, nothing. There is a man in here who's writing a history of the world. An amateur. A fool. He walks about all the time, he can't sit still. And he wears bedroom slippers. He's expecting his wife to bring him books and notes but of course she won't."

"Why not?"

"Why do you think he's here? She didn't care about his book. God knows what will happen to his notes while he's away from home."

"Ralph," said Linda tenderly.

"What?"

"Come back to me."

He turned his face away from her towards the two lunatics with their wheelbarrow.

There was a silence and then Linda said, "I'll have to go."

"Yes."

"Do you want to come to the car?"

"I don't know if I'm allowed out."

"Give me a wave then."

He didn't speak. She kissed him lightly on the lips and then left. She waved to him but he gazed back at her stonily. She seemed to be smaller than usual as she entered the car. So the strain was getting through to her. This huge plot took a lot of thinking out, no wonder she was tired. There must even be a place for the feeding rabbits and the tenuous redbreast on the branch. The car turned away in a shower of pebbles and then she was gone. The car was red as an expiring ember. Oh God, when would there be an end to this? To cut cleanly away from the world, that was what he should do. Only he didn't have the courage.

The compulsory discussions were unstructured. Sometimes someone might make a complaint, at other times there might be a general statement which would generate a debate. The scientist of whom Hugh had spoken was a tall man with a goatee beard who gave the appearance of being at home where he was, intelligent, egotistic. Hugh was there of course as was the handicapped girl, Heydrich, Lady Macbeth, and the disguised psychologist: and others. The scientist got on to the topic of the soul. Suddenly Ralph burst out impatiently, "Are we talking of the soul or of consciousness? Consciousness is what differentiates us from the animals. We carry mirrors about with us. Some time or another the leap was made, and man could see doubly, he could act and watch what he was doing at the same time."

"But surely the soul is different from that," said the scientist.

An old man with a trembling head and a trembling hand said, "Plato thinks so at any rate. He talks of the soul. Not that I can remember the exact words but I can recall doing some Greek at school."

Lady Macbeth stared dully ahead of her and so did the man whom Ralph had seen on his first day pacing up and down like a metronome.

The lady psychologist glanced rapidly at each person in turn, while another lady doctor, younger, took notes in her book.

"I'm not sure that we can equate the soul with consciousness," said the scientist, putting his pipe down on the seat beside him and stretching out his legs. "The soul is a theological thing surely. . ."

"It is a question of mirrors," said Ralph, speaking smoothly and with certainty. "One particular day man had consciousness. He called this the soul, or whatever the word was at the time. He knew that he inhabited his body like an animal but he also sensed that he had this other thing as well, by means of which he could study himself from the outside, as if he were an object. I'm not saying that he thought all this out, he sensed it. The episode in the Garden of Eden is a method of mythologizing consciousness. At first man was totally in harmony with his surroundings, later he felt himself separated from them. He wore a fig leaf but when he took the fig leaf away he discovered shame and self-consciousness."

"I still think," said the scientist, "that the soul is different from consciousness. The soul is supposed to be eternal, consciousness isn't. That's the difference surely."

"I agree," said the man with the trembling head. "Consciousness doesn't last forever. The soul is the image of God in us. Isn't that what it is supposed to be?"

The handicapped girl turned away impatiently as if she were tired of this long boring discussion. Lady Macbeth didn't change the expression on her face which was entirely dull. The metronomic man lit a cigarette and studied it speculatively. The disguised psychologist had a fixed smile on his face: he was hiding behind two other people.

"The soul is said to be eternal," said Ralph. "Of course it's meant to be eternal but that's like saying to the poor that there is a heaven. They have to have their beads of eternal glass. They are like Indians, natives. But surely we don't need to pay any attention to that."

"Why not?" said the lady psychologist, pointing at him with a long pencil which she held in her right hand. Her white hair was arranged in ridges and waves, her bright intelligent eyes were fixed on him.

"Why not? There is no proof of its existence."

"Neither is there of many other things that we accept."

"Look," said Ralph, "look at your bookshelves. They are full of books about metaphysics but what single *fact* have they uncovered equivalent to the fact that the walls of this room are painted green."

"That is another question," said the lady psychologist. "Whether the walls of this room are green or not."

"It's a fact different from the fact of the soul."

"But what about love, its eternity?" said the psychologist. "When it is said that two souls meet."

"Love? That is an affair of mirrors as well. The lover sees himself in the loved one. Love is an illusion like the soul." It was Ralph now who felt masterful. He felt that his mind moved more quickly than that of the psychologist's, or the scientist's. He felt that he was becoming master even in this place and laughed inwardly. To be avid for power even here. What a joke. The man with the trembling head who knew some Greek, who was he? He had the curious antique manners of an outdated gentleman, tentative and frail.

The handicapped girl scratched her head, another girl beside her, thin as a rake, yawned. These discussions were revolving boxes: there was no secret inside them.

"I don't agree with you about love," said the psychologist. "That it is an affair of mirrors as you put it. Do you think man is a machine?"

"Yes."

"That he has no free will?"

Oh, God, here we go again thought Ralph. "Listen," he said, "if you put a plateful of cakes all of different colours and texture in front of people at a party one will take one and one another. Why do you think that is? We are programmed by previous experience to do so."

"Programmed how far back?" said the scientist.

"As far back as the womb perhaps," said Ralph. "Free will is an illusion. You should know that as a scientist."

"I wouldn't admit that at all. Science has nothing to do with questions of free will and predestination."

"You make the same experiments and expect them to come out the same way each time. If they don't you're angry. What about Yuri Geller? Every scientist set out to prove that he was wrong, that he was breaking the laws of physics. And now we know that he was a magician. Next you'll be talking about the Bermuda Triangle, the Turin Shroud, horoscopes, that there were spacemen in early Egypt."

"Not necessarily," said the psychologist. The lady doctor in the white coat was writing furiously in her notebook. All this crap, thought Ralph, as if it had any meaning: just talk and talk and talk. . . . It's all been said over and over, there is nothing new here, just staleness.

It was like being in one of the circles of the Inferno; if only he could leave the room but he couldn't. He despised himself. He had broken his vow of silence. He looked at the clock. He should have remained like a stone in the midst of the currents and swirls of conspiracy that ebbed and flowed around him. But he hadn't reckoned with his vanity. He wanted to go to the toilet and be violently sick and spew up all his words, his ideas, his stale theories. His glib orations disgusted him.

To be loved and to love. He thought there had been a time when that had happened, when he had waited for Linda when, in her yellow dress, she would come and see him before they were married: when, if she was late or if she didn't come, the world seemed to come to a stop. He could tell the sound of her footsteps from others. But that had been long ago.

Funny that Heydrich had nothing to say. He sat there upright in his chair. What had happened to his Webley, to his negligent massacres? Was he keeping the silence of the stone man?

The silence lasted and then because men cannot bear much silence, he heard Hugh saying,

"One thing I thought to bring up, there is something wrong

with the plumbing in the toilet. It was like that when I was here four years ago and it hasn't been sorted since."

There was a muted laugh. The psychologist said, "You know what workmen are. And you know the financial restraints we have."

"I know what workers are," said Hugh. "I was one myself."

There was another muted laugh. The subject of the soul had been safely negotiated. Now one could turn to comedy. And yet Ralph wanted to discuss it more deeply, the subject of love. Was it like the cakes, were we conditioned to choose one person, or was love itself a glorious manifestation of free will, opening like a scented bouquet and conferring meaning on the whole world. It had seemed like that to him once. But now he was in chains, the world was grey and distant like Lady Macbeth's hair. She reminded him of a schoolteacher he had once had who in order to protect herself from the children had to offer them sweets. But that did not protect her.

He suddenly began to sweat and panic. He wanted more than anything to leave the room and be by himself for a while. He hung on to the legs of the chair feeling the room spinning about him. And then slowly the room steadied and he was all right again. He took out a handkerchief and wiped the sweat from his forehead. Neither the psychologist nor the note-taker was watching him at the time. They were listening to Hugh who was making some more good-humoured complaints.

The soul . . . love. . . . Where was Linda at that moment? He didn't know. And yet if he telephoned her again he would be giving in. She had cried last time and on other occasions. These tears, what were they? What did they mean? Laughter, what did that mean? Pure, mechanical exhalations. Was that right? He saw again the river and heard its quiet tranquil noise, he gazed at the deer on the hills above. The two of them had sauntered there hand in hand. Their meetings had been like a radiance of the spirit, strong as the sun that shone yellow on the hills turning them to the colour of honey. Tears rose to his eyes and he wiped them away with his hands. No, no, he must not cry, he mustn't, he had never cried in his life. That was one thing he had learned from his stepfather.

There was a burst of laughter around him. Hugh had made another pawky statement. The clock showed half-past twelve.

Now they could go for their lunch. Love could be left behind among the chairs which even now were being returned to another room. Some impulse moved the puppet Lady Macbeth towards the dining-room. Ralph joined the queue behind the man with the trembling head, and then sat at the same table with him.

"Hawkins," said the man with the trembling head, putting his hand out across the table.

"Simmons."

"I must say that I didn't agree with you but you talked well," said Hawkins.

"You seem to know Greek," said Ralph.

"My father was a doctor. He was a great man. Great personality. He stayed in the same district all his life but he was a tremendous personality. He taught me Greek." Hawkins thought for a while and then said, "He committed suicide."

"I'm sorry," said Ralph. And then. "What did you used to do yourself?"

"Me? I was in charge of a scientific laboratory. Investigating various chemicals. I was to be shifted to England but I retired instead. I didn't want to go to England. I was to be merged with a lot of other laboratories."

He leaned forward confidentially. "I fell ill and I attended this Pakistani doctor. And he told the psychologist that I was going to commit suicide. I had never said that to him at all." And his eyes flared with a brief anger.

"I have depressions, of course, since my wife died, but I never at any time said that I was going to commit suicide."

His hands shook as he took a piece of bread from the plate in front of him. "I must say, that your talk today reminded me of my father. He was an atheist you see. He didn't believe in the soul."

"Do you?"

"In the soul? I don't know. I often think that someone with as powerful a personality as my father had will never die. Then again in practical terms nothing ever dies. There's an exchange of energies."

All the time he was speaking his head was shaking uncontrollably.

"Tell me," said Ralph, "do you think we can ever tell what is truth."

"Tell what is truth? What do you mean?"

163

"I mean here we are talking to each other and we can't tell what either of us is really thinking. There's no way of knowing. Words don't mean anything, do they? They are disguises for the truth. They are what we say when we are thinking of something else."

"I suppose so," said Hawkins slowly. A piece of bread stuck to the left side of his mouth. "My father always told the truth. To tell the truth and be damned, he'd always say. People respected him. He was a big bluff man. I'm not sure whether telling the truth always works but people admired him for it. My mother said he should have been more tactful. I remember him saying to a patient, "Aren't you dead yet, man?" The odd thing was that they loved him for it."

"That's not exactly what I mean," said Ralph. "Look, is there no way of finding out what goes on behind the face."

"None," said Hawkins with finality.

"Then," said Ralph, "we may live in a world of perpetual betrayal."

"Yes. You find the same in the natural world. Animals disguise themselves so that they won't be eaten. Take the chameleon, for example. But there are thousands of examples. That of course might cause depression."

"What might?"

"The strain of keeping up a disguise. Some of course are more natural liars than others. My father said that a lot of his patients were liars. If they told the truth they might be better off. There's a woman I used to know who kept up the pretence of having been a landowner in Kenya. She had never been to Kenya in her life. She would talk of her doctor in Harley Street. She lived in a room and kitchen."

"Why did your father commit suicide?"

"I don't know. He hanged himself. He used to say that one had no reason for living if one had no future. He was referring to his patients. They had no future and they still lived."

"Did he believe that he himself had no future?"

"I don't know. His suicide came as a great surprise to everyone. That very day he had been issuing pills. His diary was full. Everyone loved him. Sometimes when he came into a patient's house he would start dancing."

"I don't think I'll ever write again," said Ralph suddenly.

"Are you a writer then?"

164

"Yes. I'm a novelist but you won't have read any of my books. The fact is I can't concentrate. And another thing. I don't believe in words any more. They're no different from spit. No, they're worse than spit, they're dangerous. I'm sick of them. They betrayed me. If you live long enough everything betrays you, even the earth itself. Even the things that are dearest to you. Where is there evidence in the universe for love?"

"Love? In the universe?"

"Yes, that truism love. Everything is the ego magnified."

"I think I loved my wife," said Hawkins quietly. "I think I loved my wife and my father."

"You mean you admired him."

"I'm not sure. I think I loved him. And my wife too. I often think of her. She would have gone with me to England even though she would have hated it. That is, if I had wanted her to. I used to invite some of my friends in to talk. She didn't understand what we were talking about but it didn't seem to matter to her. She was Irish. She showed me a translation of an Irish poem once. It was about a dead wife written by her husband. It went,

> Half of my side you were, half of my seeing,
> half of my walking you were, half of my hearing.

Only the other day I was reading of a woman who was going to have a baby and who had cancer. If she had the baby she knew that she would die. She sacrificed herself for the baby."

The handicapped girl with the flat white face leaned over to take the plates. I hate this place, thought Ralph, I hate it. I don't understand anything. It was as if his mind were breaking, revealing gaps here and there through clouds. Was love what Heydrich and the handicapped girl felt when they walked hand in hand through the grounds? Was love what the birds felt on their engraved courses? Curse you, he thought, all you unimaginative ones, all you who can't put yourselves in the places of the others, all you who trample through the sacred groves with your heavy boots, curse you, my marble-faced stepfather.

He rose abruptly from the table and went into the lounge. There was a scatter of newspapers and magazines and he picked one up and, after a while, dropped it. Opposite him lying on the floor was a record player with a number of records beside it, like large black cards without purpose. There was a chess-board and a draughts-board. When the 'psychologist' came in he said to him,

"Would you like a game of chess?"

"I don't play," said the psychologist slowly.

"I'll teach you to play."

"Well, I'm no very clever. I dinna ken if I'm able," said the psychologist relapsing suddenly into dialect.

"Of course you're able. It's quite simple."

He laid a chess-board out on the table and arranged the pieces on it. "Now watch," he said. "These are the pawns. And this is the king and that's the queen. That is the rook and this is the bishop and this is the knight. The pawns can move forward one piece at a time or, on the first move, two squares. The rook can move any number of squares horizontally or vertically. The queen is the most powerful piece on the board and can move any number of squares, diagonally, horizontally or vertically. The bishop can move diagonally any number of squares. The king can only move one square at a time. The purpose of the game is to put the king in check."

The psychologist gazed down at the board while Ralph was talking, his brow wrinkled.

"The object of the game is to gain control of the centre," said Ralph. "Now I'll make the first move. What are you going to do then in answer to my pawn move?"

The psychologist moved a pawn on his left flank.

"That's not a good move," said Ralph. "Why did I tell you it wasn't?"

"Well, I canna . . . should I have moved it this way?" And he indicated the diagonal line.

"No, that's not it. The object is to gain control of the centre. So there's no point in moving that pawn. What do you want to do instead?"

"I dinna ken."

"Move one of the centre pawns. That'll free your bishop, do you see?"

Ralph on his second move brought another pawn to protect his first one.

"Do you see that?" he asked. "You can't take that pawn while I have this one here. Pawns take diagonally."

166

The psychologist moved one of his own pawns forward and tried to take Ralph's pawn frontally.

So you're at it, thought Ralph, you think I'm going to imagine that you're as stupid as that. You're trying to pretend that you're not really a psychologist but a country bumpkin.

"No," he said, "you can't do that. You take diagonally. You can't take frontally. What are you going to do now?" he asked, replacing the pawn. The psychologist moved his pawn again frontally.

"You can't do that. I just told you," said Ralph. "You take diagonally."

And he replaced the board as it was at the beginning. "Look," he said, "let's begin again." And he went through all the moves of all the pieces while the psychologist listened, brow wrinkled. You're not deceiving me, thought Ralph.

But still he couldn't teach him how to play. He moved pawns diagonally, bishops frontally, knights at random. It was almost as if he were being deliberately obtuse.

You can't be so stupid, thought Ralph, gritting his teeth. No one can. All this is a disguise. Even an idiot could understand what I've told you. After a while he gave up. The psychologist was smiling at him and shaking his head.

"It's nae use," he said, "I'm too stupid."

Damn you, thought Ralph. You're watching me all the time. Chess isn't as difficult as that.

And he stared at the psychologist. What are you really. What is going on behind your forehead? For a moment there I thought you were genuinely stupid but I know you're not. It's not the stupid who try to kill themselves, is it?

"Why did you take the aspirins?" he asked suddenly.

"I dinna ken. I stay with my brither-in-law and his wife. I was working very hard. Maybe that's what it was."

"Do you still see the rays?"

"No so bad now. They're no so bad."

"What do they look like?"

"Whit?"

"The rays?"

"They're like rays. They're bright."

Ralph felt impatient with this man's mind or his adopted mask. "Do they come and see you, your brother-in-law and his wife?"

"Aye. They're very good to me."

"That's good. How many sheep do you have on your farm?"

"Aboot fower hundred."

"Four hundred."

"Ay, that's what we dae. Sheep farming."

"Is it hard work?"

"Depends on the season, ye ken."

The man had an accent, rural certainly. He must be a real actor, he must have practised the authenticity of his accent for months. Oh, he was good right enough, he never put a foot wrong and yet he hadn't learnt chess. But that would be part of the disguise. Maybe however he had overdone his stupidity.

"Can I get your books in the library?" said the psychologist seriously.

"I suppose so," said Ralph. "If you want to. Do you read a lot?"

"No much. I listen to the wireless."

"Do you watch tv?"

"No much. I see the rays."

Ralph packed the pieces away in the box provided. He was beginning to get the feeling of unreality again. He suddenly got up and left the room, walking along the corridor past the office. He lay down fully clothed on his bed and tried to sleep.

That evening Ronny was moved out of the ward because he wouldn't take his pills and he was becoming more and more obstreperous.

"I don't care," he said defiantly. "It'll be a gig."

"Why don't you do what people tell you," said Hugh, lighting another of his cigarettes and padding restlessly about the ward.

"I don't want to."

"What do you mean you don't want to? You know this is the best ward, don't you? I think you're stupid."

"I'm not stupid, old man," said Ronny with sudden aggression.

"Well then what are you? You could have stayed here and then you could have gone home shortly."

"I know that."

"Why don't you do what they tell you then?"

"I don't know. I'll leave you my orangeade."

"I don't want your orangeade. You can keep your orangeade." And Hugh turned away angrily. "I can't make head or tail of you."

"You haven't got a head or a tail, old man," said Ronny, laughing boisterously, and hardly able to stop.

"There you go again laughing. What are you laughing at?" said Hugh, angry in his turn.

"The old man hasn't a head or a tail," said Ronny, still hysterically laughing.

"Och, you can go then," said Hugh, disgustedly. And he padded out of the room.

"What's wrong with him?" said Ronny. "He can't take a joke."

"Well, why aren't you taking your pills?" said Ralph.

"Because they make you impotent."

"And why don't you get up in the morning?"

"What's there to get up for? All we do is sit around here all day. And we have to make our beds. I used to drive my stepfather batty. I never made my bed in the morning. He was in the navy and he didn't like that. He used to beat me up but I never made my bed. And I used to put pin-ups on the walls of my room. He didn't like that either." And he giggled hysterically at the memory. "When I get out of here I'll do him. I'm taller than him. He won't push me around."

"You should go and tell the charge nurse that you'll take your pills."

"That old bag. No, I won't. She's got VD."

"What?"

"She's got VD." And he burst out laughing again, bending over almost double till finally he got his breath back. "I don't like people with VD."

"She hasn't."

"Of course she has. You can tell at once. Do you know they took a fellow from the next room away. I saw him on the stretcher. He was hitting the walls with his fists. They can't keep me here, he was shouting." And he began to laugh again. "And there's another fellow here in a coma. Did you know that. He's been in a coma for three weeks. This is a great place. They should bring my stepfather here."

He looked around him. "Well I think that's everything. Where's the old man gone? I should like to say cheerio to him." And he began to chant,

> "Where has the old man gone
> where has the old man gone
> where has the old man gone,
> he's gone to take his pills.

Did you notice how he walks? He slides along the floor as if he was on wheels. He never lifts his feet, did you notice that? You'd think he was a mouse. The old man is a mouse, the old man is a mouse."

At that moment Hugh returned from his restless peregrination and Ronny said, "We were just talking about you. You're a mouse, you're a mouse."

"Aw, shut up. You should have done what I told you, you big idiot. You should have obeyed the nurses. And you should have got out of bed in the mornings, instead of lying there like a crab with diarrhoea."

"A crab with diarrhoea? Did you hear that? Did you hear what the old man said?" And again he laughed hysterically. "I'll miss you, old man."

"All right then, you'll miss me. So you should. I gave you good advice. But you've got wormwood in your head."

"Look after the old man," said Ronny to Ralph. "Make sure he gets plenty of cheese. He's a mouse, he's a mouse, he's a mouse on wheels."

And he turned away. Ralph noticed that he had left his record 'Breakdown' behind him and nearly shouted after him but in the end didn't. There was a woman in a blue uniform washing the corridor outside the room. Ronny stepped right into the water, waving as he went.

The days were endlessly boring. Sometimes between meals Ralph would walk about the room, sometimes lie on his bed. Since the unsatisfactory chess session he hadn't tried to teach the psychologist — whose name was Tom — again. He couldn't concentrate on the newspapers, couldn't read books, and he felt that if he stayed much longer in the institution he would really go out of his mind. After all there was no reason why he should be

170

here, there was nothing wrong with him, he was the victim of a plot. The days passed like years. Ronny was replaced by a slightly older youth with anorexia nervosa who wouldn't eat any food, and when he was enticed to the dining-room ran away again. He laughed in the same high giggling manner but his relationship with Hugh was not similar. Ralph thought it was like being in a barrack room, the same monotony, the same pointless endurance, the same compulsory commerce with other people.

One day he and Tom went to the canteen: this was the first time either had been out of the hospital, even though it only meant crossing perhaps a hundred yards of grass and climbing some steps. The canteen was close to the worst wards, and when Ralph entered it he saw people of a different kind from those in his own ward. They were more like the two he had seen putting the leaves in the wheelbarrow. Their faces were blank and white like turnips, their heads crew cut, and their eyes threateningly focussed.

One of them buttonholed him and said, "Do you think the Government is in hospital? Do you think Maggie Thatcher's in hospital?"

He backed away muttering, "They could be, they could be."

"I think they're in hospital," the man insisted.

I wonder why Tom brought me here, thought Ralph, for it had been Tom's idea. He must have had a reason for it. He said he wanted sweets but maybe there was another hidden reason.

When they had crossed the ground among the autumn leaves and the cold wind, he had felt an unaccountable sadness as if he had come to the end of the world, as if he would never leave this place, as if he was slowly dying. The purest uttermost pain must be like this, this exile from the world in elegiac autumn.

Sitting at a table in the canteen a large man was trying to cram a cake into his mouth with both hands. Ralph made himself watch him, made himself almost experience, taste the soggy mess, gulp it hungrily. It seemed to him that his writing demanded this, otherwise he would be a coward. The man with the cake succeeded in transforming his whole face into a dead white colour as if he were a ghost or a snowman.

Tom bought his sweets and they left the canteen together, descending the steps.

"I live over there," said Tom, suddenly pointing. "Do you see that farm? That's where I live."

171

"I didn't know you lived around here," said Ralph.

"Ay, that's where my brither-in-law's farm is."

Was it true then, thought Ralph. Was it true that Tom was exactly what he said he was. Why else would he have pointed to that particular building in this particular place?

Or was that too part of the plot? Could it be?

"There between the trees you can see the sheep," said Tom. Tom could easily have run away home, so close he was. And yet he walked docilely and obediently to the house and entered by the front door.

"Was that your wife the other day?" he asked Ralph.

"Yes."

"Does she drive a long way?"

"About a hundred miles."

"She comes quite often."

"Yes."

"I was talking to her the other day. She's a nice lady."

"Are you married yourself?"

"No."

"You stay with your brother-in-law?"

"Yes."

The last time she had come he had been vicious to her, told her not to come back. She had left weeping. If he was to suffer so much pain why should he not tell her to stay away? On the other hand when he asked her to stay away he suffered pain too. It didn't matter what he did, he suffered pain.

"I'm going to Glasgow tomorrow," said Tom, "to get the electric treatment."

"Are you sure that's wise?"

"I dinna ken. I have to go. I'm going down in an ambulance." A trio of nurses passed hand in hand like a bevy of birds.

He had told Linda that he didn't love her, that everything was a pretence, that love didn't exist, that hell was other people. And yet after she had driven off in her car he had wanted to call her back. What if this time she took him at his word, what if she never came back again? He imagined her steadily driving away from him, saying to herself, This is no good, how can I continue like this. All I get is abuse. On the other hand she was going to her true love, the Irish psychologist, and the two of them would drink wine together and make jokes about him.

"Tom," he said, using the name for the first time as if it were a real one. "Do you know anything about a psychologist in the hospital? He speaks Irish, I mean with an Irish accent."

"No, the one I go to doesn't have an Irish accent. Anyway it's a woman I go to."

Ralph hated the Irishman with a bitter hatred, he hated his poise, his suave decorum, he thought of him as his most bitter rival. To be like him, so assured, so professional, so relaxed — but he couldn't be. Of course Linda would prefer such a man to Ralph, it was only natural. Though intelligent, he wasn't silent or élitist. He wondered where they had met, and how the plot had been elaborated. He must be a very good psychologist to create such a ramification of mazes.

The following morning, at the usual meeting, the lady psychologist asked the other patients for help with a young girl who had come in as a voluntary patient. She was very thin and suffering from anorexia nervosa. She had just had a baby and believed that people were spying on her and trying to take the baby away.

"You must really look after yourself for the sake of the baby," the scientist was the first to say. "After all if something happens to you what will happen to the baby? You should stay here till you are well."

"I won't stay here. I've changed my mind. I don't like this place." The girl wore a short skirt and smiled provocatively.

"Where is your baby now?" said Hugh.

"My mother is looking after it. It was her who persuaded me to come in here but I can see now that she wants the baby for herself. She said they wouldn't keep me long."

"Well, you may not be in long," said the scientist tapping his pipe on the side of his chair.

"I think I will be in a long time if I stay. People are trying to make me eat and I don't like eating."

"Who were the spies you were talking about?" the handicapped girl stuttered.

"Everybody. My baby is illegitimate. People were talking about me at the bus stops, in the shops, everywhere. Old bags. They wouldn't stop talking about me. Even the traffic wardens. They were waving their arms and pointing to me."

"Come off it," said Hugh. "They would have been doing traffic duty. Traffic wardens are always waving their arms. That's what they're for." He turned round to the company. "I was on holiday one time among the teuchters and I was driving through this town and this traffic warden waved me on. But at the same time he was nodding his head from side to side. I didn't know what to do so I stayed where I was. He came up to me and he said, 'Why aren't you driving on?' 'Well,' I said, 'I didn't know what to do. You're waving me on with your hands and yet you're nodding your head from side to side.' 'Ach,' he said, 'don't you know your Highland Code. It should be the hands you should be watching and not the head.'"

Some of the group laughed but the girl remained stony faced as if she didn't see the point of the joke. Then after a while she said, "Are you trying to say something about my head?"

"Of course he's not," said the scientist placatingly. "He was just telling a joke."

"Well, he should keep his jokes to himself. And you too what are you laughing at," she said, turning to another girl whom Ralph had only seen once before. "What are you f...... laughing at?"

"Stop f...... shouting at me," said the girl angrily.

"Now, now, calm down both of you," said the psychologist who had been sitting quietly listening. "The point is, Diana, what are we going to do about you? For your own sake and the sake of your baby you should really accept treatment. It isn't reasonable to think that people are spying on you."

"They are f...... spying on me. Do you think I'm a headcase? They talk about me all the time. I can't go out of the house. I can't even take my baby out in the pram. These f...... old bags are always coming to have a look at him."

For the first time the man with the trembling head spoke. "Women always do that," he said, in his civilized scholarly voice. "They always bend down and look at babies."

"What do you know about it, you old fart," said the girl angrily.

"Now please, Diana, that's no way to talk," said the psychologist. "We're only trying to help you."

"You're trying to get me to eat and I don't want to. I've changed my mind. I shouldn't have come in here in the first place."

174

All the time Ralph was listening. He wanted to give some advice but he didn't know what to say. The girl, he could see, was miserable and unhappy and unwell. On the other hand her statements were making him uneasy. Why did she think that traffic wardens were laughing at her? They were only directing the traffic, surely.

Was this then a part of the conspiracy against himself? Had the girl been put up to this, to repeat his own story in a different way, with different characters? Still, if she was an actress she was very good, very authentic. And her bad language was the first he had heard used in the hospital. He passed his hand across his forehead, thinking hard. The girl certainly was very thin and it seemed to him that she hadn't been eating. For a moment there he felt as if these were real people and not a theatrical group: it was the bad language that had done it, for everybody seemed to be as shocked as he himself was, and the scholarly trembling man was staring down at the floor as if he had been mortally hurt. Unless of course the girl belonged to a more real, harsher school of acting than the others and they were now intent on forcing the issue with himself, considering that he was taking so long to break down.

"Don't you love your baby?" he heard himself ask.

"Of course I f...... love my baby. What sort of question is that? But they won't let me have him. My mother takes him away from me. I'm not going to harm him. I'm not going to poison him."

"Well, then, why don't you take treatment. Do as you're told. Take your pills."

"I told you. I'm not taking the pills. I don't want pills. I want to go home. What is happening to my baby while I'm in here. That's what I want to know. Maybe my mother has run away with him and I won't be able to trace her."

And she began to scream and wail, rocking from side to side and clutching at her thin body.

Stop, stop, stop, Ralph almost shouted aloud. Stop this at once, you're hurting my head.

And without thinking he rushed out of the lounge and ran along to his room clutching his head. He lay down on the bed. The room was spinning around him and his mouth was forming soundless screams. His head was bursting, he was sweating profusely. As he lay on the bed he heard someone coming after him. He had a glimpse of a pale face, a uniform, and then he was being given a pill, and put below the blankets. In a short while he fell asleep.

He woke up in the morning at the usual time. Hugh was already out of his bed and padding about the room in his dressing-gown. The yellow light of the electric bulb was cast over the ward. Ralph put on his dressing-gown and made his bed.

"Brilliant," he said glancing down at it. "Isn't it brilliant. Can't I make a brilliant bed?"

"You're learning," said Hugh, considering the bed like a scholar considering a manuscript. "Another six months and you should be all right."

Ralph laughed. He knew that Hugh was joking. Wasn't it a tremendous thing that he should know that? Tom was sitting on his bed in the corner smiling, now and again blinking his eyes as he habitually did.

"About your book," said Ralph. "I can give you a *Writers' and Artists' Yearbook.*"

"What's that?"

"It tells you the addresses of publishers. I'll get my wife to bring it in to you."

"Thanks," said Hugh.

"And today I'll have a bath," said Ralph. "Isn't that great? Little adventures all the time."

The last time he had had a bath he had panicked because he couldn't get the door open. And when he went to the toilet he never closed the door: it was as if he was afraid of being locked in a box.

What was the source of this joy that he felt? It was pouring all round him like the yellow light. He felt lightheaded as if he could fly. Today too he was seeing the psychologist again. So that was two things, the bath and the psychologist. They would make his day, he smiled ironically. He padded along the corridor to retrieve his razor from the office. The charge nurse handed it over saying, "Feeling okay today?"

"I'm feeling great," he answered.

When he looked into the mirror in the bathroom he saw that the apelike expression had disappeared from his face. To the right of him Heydrich was gazing contentedly into his own area of glass. Ralph was no longer frightened of him, no longer frightened to be in the bathroom with any of the others. Before, he had thought they might attack him. This grave joy, where had it come from? He wanted to talk to somebody, to anybody, to share his joy. It was as if he had risen from the tomb and his shroud had fallen away like expended wings.

"And how is Heydrich this morning?" he asked gaily.

"Fine," said the tall fair haired 'Nazi' drawing the razor down his throat and sweeping the foam away in billowing waves.

"And what are you going to do today?"

"I have orders to write. That'll keep me going for a while. I must get rid of more of these bloody Jews."

"What are you going to do with them?"

"I'm going to machine-gun the bastards."

"I see," said Ralph, feeling the room spin around him, and the joy leaving him. But when he had got back to the ward the joy had returned again. His mind was moving in free leaps; Linda hadn't touched the telephone book after all. It was he himself who had torn it up, though he couldn't remember having done so. And these obscene messages which he had found in his books and his diary, he must have written them himself. He, also, it must have been who had disarranged the pages of his novel. The Irish psychologist was what he had always been, an Irish psychologist. Why shouldn't psychologists be Irish: they had as much right to be Irish as any other nationality.

When he arrived back in his room Hugh said, "I forgot to tell you. I'm getting out Thursday."

"You must be pleased," said Ralph.

"Yes, my wife's coming to collect me. I have a lot to do when I get home. All my notes to arrange. And then I'll have to see my sons to find out how the business is going. I've got a share in it. I visit them every second Sunday, usually, and have my dinner with them."

"How's your concentration?"

"Not so good. I'm working on a chapter on the Trade Unions at the moment. It takes a lot of reading." He looks so old-fashioned, thought Ralph, like a superannuated officer from the First World War with his ghostly moustache. And he's so meticulous with everything, his leather shaving case, his bed: all must be neat and tidy. When the soul dies we become machines.

We move like machines, jerky, remorseless. Our eyes lose their human shine and our faces become like those of chimpanzees.

The soul, what was it? It had shone like a halo above the animal nibbling at his cloud of fruit. On the other hand, was it the soul? Was it not simply consciousness? But what was the source of this joy, this coming back to himself as a stranger to his own house at last, a tide returning to a shore that had been long unfamiliar? Was this consciousness that pervaded his whole body as sap does a tree or was it more than that, did it have the unique signature of holiness? He wanted to extend himself everywhere, to shout, to tell an immense and priceless secret. He studied his bed again. No, it wasn't quite right. The final flick of the blanket like a tail had been omitted. He imitated Hugh and corrected it.

"I'm becoming a real artist at this," he said.

Through the parted curtains he could see the dawn reddening the sky, and he could hear the twitter of birds. The sun was beginning to force its way through the clouds with steady remorselessness. The stars like pills were being overwhelmed by that rawer stronger light. He could just make out a cat padding across the wet grass. He felt the material of his silk dressing-gown — the one Linda had bought for him — with wonderment. It passed like water through his hands.

After lunch he and Tom helped the woman who was washing the dishes. The dishes were put in a machine and then dried. He and Tom spent half an hour on them before they went to the lounge for their pills. It was a simple machine but he was delighted that he could operate it.

"Look at the food that's left," said the small woman in the blue uniform. "Some of them hardly eat a thing. Hardly a thing." And she nodded her head as she walked to and fro in the kitchen.

"The waste," she said. "Did you see that fellow? He put his head in at the door and ran away again. Anorexia nervosa," she said wisely. "That's what the doctors call it. Nothing but skin and bone on them."

"Why do they do it?" asked Ralph as he dried a plate.

"You tell me. It's mostly girls. They want to keep their figures, that's what I think. I'm slimming myself, but I know when to stop. I watch my tatties and my bread and my sugar. I just have a coffee when I come out in the morning. And no cakes. I have a big meal at night though. It's not natural to slim as much as they do, and that boy is as bad as the girls. It isn't often you see it in boys, mind you. My own boys were the opposite, couldn't get enough food. And they would say to visitors, We're starving. I felt so mortified." Her voice became more confidential. "Listen, you wouldn't believe this. I had a visitor the other week, my sister it was, Jane, that's my sons' aunt. Very pernickety she is, toffee-nosed, very madamy, and Sam, that's one of my sons, doesn't like her. I offered her a sherry. 'And what do you drink, Sam?' she said. 'Coke,' he said. But I could see he was mad at her. 'Coke,' she says. 'And do you really like coke?' She talks to him as if he was a wee boy and he hates it. I tried to get him out of the room to wash the dishes but he never washes dishes. 'No,' he said. 'And why don't you like it then?' ''Cos it makes me fart.'"

And she went into fits of laughter, joined by Ralph and Tom. In between bouts of laughter she muttered wiping her eyes, "You should have seen her face. She's so proud, you see. The sherry nearly fell out of her hand. But these boys, you'll never know what they're going to say next. They make me so ashamed. Sam used to sit in the garden like a Hindu when he was in university. He wore dirty sandals all the time. Mind you, he's smart, I'll say that for him. But this won't pay the rent. Many thanks." Tom and Ralph folded up the towels, put them in the drawer, and went for their pills.

In the lounge, while he was waiting for his pills, he sat beside the girl who had checked in as a voluntary patient.

"Can I talk to you?" he said quietly.

"If you want," said the girl in a hostile manner.

"It's just that I wanted to tell you what had happened to me. I thought everyone was spying on me. I thought my wife had written obscene messages all over my books. And that she had torn the telephone book in two. I had the idea that she had plotted to send me to the hospital."

"How do you know she didn't?"

"I just know."

"How do you know?" For a moment the nightmare returned, hovering with its black wings on the edge of his mind but he pushed it away with all his might.

179

"I just know," he repeated. "It wouldn't be reasonable that the hospital nurses, doctors, taxi drivers, psychologists, would all be involved in a plot. It's not reasonable that traffic wardens should be talking about you."

"But they are talking about me. They think I'm a criminal."

"Why?"

"Why what?"

"Why do they think you're a criminal?"

"Because I'm not married, that's why."

"But that doesn't make you a criminal."

"It does to them."

"Listen," said Ralph urgently. "You're wrong, you know. You're making a mistake. They cured me in here. I took my pills and they cured me. One day you wake up and you know that it's all been a bad dream."

"What was a dream?"

"The idea that people were spying on me."

Suddenly the girl spoke in a hard voice. "Who sent you to talk to me? Is this part of the plot as well?"

"No one sent me."

"I know somebody sent you. They're all against me because I don't eat my food. Well, I'm not staying here. And one of the girls stole some of my clothes. I'll get the f...... bitch. She took a scarf of mine. But she's not getting away with it. And there's another thing, when they weighed me they told me the wrong weight. I'm getting out of here."

"I'm not spying on you," said Ralph desperately. "I'm trying to help you. I want you to get well. I got well."

"How do you know?"

"How do I know what?"

"Like how do you know that you weren't well before and you're ill now. How do you know?"

Her sharp belligerent intelligence pierced him but he knew that he must hang on: he must cling to his joy. His joy told him that all was well, his misery had vanished like a cloud. The people in the lounge had all swum back into focus again. The room was real, its occupants were not actors, there was no longer a threat.

"I know," he said, "because I feel happy."

"Happy."

Her eyes on his were hard and hostile, and bitter as if he were her enemy.

"Why should I listen to you? Jim told me that he'd marry me but he didn't. He changed his mind. Over and over he said that he would marry me. Give me it, he'd say, give me it, I'll marry you, I swear I will. And he pawed me all over and he breathed like a pig. But he never married me. He never came to see me."

"I see," said Ralph. Her pallor was poignant and childlike. Tears were brimming from her eyes. How many of these girls he had seen, on streets late at night, with their cracked handbags in the yellow fallen light, walking in pairs, giggling their high virginal giggles.

"Listen," he said, from the very centre of his care, of his joy.

"Get away from me, old man," said the girl. "Or I'll tell Snooty face. Get the f...... hell away from me." And her voice rose hysterically. Ralph got to his feet quickly and moved over to where Tom was sitting cradling his coffee cup in his hands as if he was warming them. The following day he was going to Glasgow to have the operation to his head.

"Come on out for a walk," he said. They made their way along a road beside which were fields and houses: a house that had once been a nunnery and was now a Nurses' Home. Tom knew the area well as he had been brought up close to it, after being born in Aberdeenshire. They opened and shut gates and strolled between tall red foxgloves like burning spires in the cold raw wind. It was strange to smell the scent of flowers again, to have the freedom of the air: it was as if already in reality he were leaving the hospital behind him.

There was an immense silence and purity everywhere, like Easter, like the resurrection. Cows gazed at them with absent eyes, chewing green blades of grass.

"I think you'll be oot quicker than me," said Tom.

"What makes you think that?"

"They told me I might be fower or five weeks after my electric treatment. They say it'll mak me dizzy for a few days."

Now that he could see properly the delineaments of the world he could understand that after all Tom was not a psychologist but a rural man, and an authentic non-chess player. His accent was explained by the fact that he had not been born in the area.

For the first time Ralph felt that he might be allowed home. The mountains, flowers, animals, fields, were not alien to him but natural. They were not inconceivable gifts but ordinary and fixed in their places, to be accepted. They did not represent an infinite yearning of the spirit towards the unattainable.

A large brown butterfly swam past and settled on the leaf of a tree, swaying and drifting. My mind didn't make that, he said to himself, it is out there, drunken, dizzy. He saw some rabbits playing in a cold field.

When they were returning after their short walk he could see the institution for the first time in full focus from a distance. It looked like an academy, like a school built of grey elegant stone. It had towers and columns and a lovely porch. It seemed at peace, classical, exact. Odd that it should seem so, he thought. But perhaps the palaces of Greece were the same, not apparently resounding with the cries of tragedy, with the griefs of heroes and heroines as through tragedy they made the painful evolutionary climb away from their gods.

"Well, here we are then," said Tom.

"So you're all right now," said the psychologist flanked by her nurses.

"Yes."

"Not feeling you're being spied on, or were ever spied on?"

"No. I feel fine."

"None of this nonsense of your telephone book being torn by your wife?"

"No, I realize now it must have been myself."

"And no nonsense of anyone having interfered with your papers?"

"None. I must have done that myself too."

"And this boy Ronny, is that his name, wasn't put there deliberately?"

"No."

"I see. And how do you feel? Appetite good?"

"Yes."

"Sleeping well?"

"Yes."

"And your wife? How do you feel about your wife?"

"I love her. And I'm sorry. She was put under a great strain."

"Good. If all goes well I think you should be out of here in two or three days."

"Thank you. And I'm very sorry for all the trouble I've caused."

"You couldn't help yourself."

"I suppose not."

"But it is quite clear what happened. You were overworking. And you felt symptoms of overwork before your breakdown, didn't you."

"I used to burst out in sudden sweats. For no reason at all. And I felt mentally exhausted even when I was on holiday."

"And you realize that I'm a psychologist and that these are real nurses."

"Of course. I've been so stupid."

It occurred to him while the psychologist was talking that reality was far more fragile than he had thought, that whatever picture of reality one chose could be corroborated by information pouring in and being filtered, that a madman was the most rigorously logical of all beings, not at all scatterbrained but rather remorselessly reasonable. He wanted to discuss this with the psychologist, but when he looked at her as if for the first time, he saw a grossly overworked woman whose eyes were filled with pain, who herself tapped on the desk obsessively with a pencil. This was no infallible goddess, this was a human being just like himself.

"Thank you," he said again, "thank you for curing me."

He knew suddenly why Hamlet needed Horatio as a witness, why Horatio had to be left behind to tell the truth as he saw it, to explain the extraordinary pattern of events, the murders, the accidents. The most terrible thing of all would be to be in a world without witnesses, a Robinson Crusoe on an island. That in a sense was what he had been.

And another thought occurred to him; he, the novelist, rundown, struggling with his book, face to face with the bareness and meagreness of his material, had deliberately created a plot, a novel, in the real world, had interfered with reality in order to invent new events, strange and perilous, had put his immortal soul on the line, had thrown a gauntlet at sanity in the interests of art. The observer had gambled with his own soul.

"Well, then," said the psychologist brightly, "that's it. I shall probably see you again before you leave. Keep up the good work."

"Thank you," he said. He walked out with the same joy as he had felt before. In a short while he would be free, he would be at home again, he would see his office and his wife. He wanted to see her again as soon as possible to tell her how much he loved her. Love was what saved us from the demonic nature of reality. Together the lovers are common witnesses of the world.

But there was something else that bothered him too. He had not reached the uttermost limits, he had not visited the really mad, he had not seen them in their meagre cages, he had not sought out their discords to make sense of them.

Was he therefore a failure as a novelist? Could he face that final place without harmony? He looked out of the window and saw that the man he had seen the first day in his room had entered the hospital from outside and was pacing up and down. Then he noticed that he was waiting for a car. Was he being taken on a day trip somewhere? He saw the man's wife speaking to him and the man himself, perhaps her husband, her brother, staring straight ahead of him through the windscreen silently, his lips not moving.

The autumn leaves were blowing about the strange tree with the pink petals. No one had yet told him what kind of tree it was.

Linda, my love, he thought, how much I made you suffer. I must atone for this. I must tell you of my love. I must change, must enter the ordinary world. I must ascend into it.

It was the day of his departure. All morning he had been pacing up and down his room and then up and down the corridor. The scientist had already left the hospital, waving at him with his pipe like Einstein. Heydrich and the handicapped girl strolled to the canteen for sweets, cigarettes. Hugh had gone home but the boy who wouldn't eat was still in the ward and so was Tom who would be in for a few weeks yet. Ronny had not yet come back from the extreme place.

Any moment now he would see Linda's car. And then, as he watched for it, for its brisk red flame, he saw the two lunatics spearing the leaves and placing them in the barrow. They looked up once or twice and it seemed to him that they were staring at him with their unwrinkled brows.

He had again the feeling that he had failed them, failed himself, that he had not suffered enough. Must I enter the final rooms of unreason, is that asked of me, he questioned himself. And it seemed to him that happiness was what he had avoided because he hadn't thought he deserved it. Not finding grace he had sought its equivalent through work: every book had been a justification of himself, a gift he had brought pleadingly to his stepfather. "If you want books I can write them for you: you couldn't do that, so I am better than you. I am a creator: you are only a parasite. You are a worm, a book worm." That icy face didn't even break into a smile when he brought him book after book. More, more, more, it demanded.

Even while he was thinking this he was imagining Linda speeding towards him across winding intricate roads, past lochs and woods, arrowing towards him in the fine silvery day. Her faithfulness now astonished him, made him proud. Her love had been great indeed. In spite of everything, tiredness, perplexity, grief, she had stayed with him to the very end. As he stood there in his phantom cloak of stone and sorrow and joy he swayed and rocked.

And then out of the indifferent day the red car came, and he saw her quite small crouched figure behind the wheel, gripping it tightly, her face pale and tiny as a shell. He ran along the corridor to the front door carrying his case in his hand. He was running past the office and they were shouting "Good luck" to him, and then he was walking towards the car. For a moment he stood under the tree in the shelter of its flaming petals, watching the two men lifting the leaves on sharp prongs. Then with a final gesture as if of repudiation he turned away towards the car, the door of which Linda had opened. She ran towards him and they swayed and rocked in each other's arms. Joy was flooding his mind and body. His witness was with him. Love was what moved the stars and the other planets and kept us steady in the stormy astronomy of reality.

He looked back. Ronny was waving towards him from the window. He must just have been returned, promoted to a higher circle. He pointed out Ronny to Linda and they both waved to him. Then Ronny's face disappeared as if it had been an illusion.

He clutched Linda briefly. Reality was what one had to cling to: one should not take chances with it. The stone cloak of duty fell away from his shoulders. At that moment it did not bother him if he never wrote again.